York St John
ⁿy and Inf

Pⁱ

Global Issues

Resource Books for Teachers
series editor Alan Maley

Global Issues

Ricardo Sampedro
Susan Hillyard

OXFORD
UNIVERSITY PRESS

OXFORD

UNIVERSITY PRESS

Great Clarendon Street, Oxford OX2 6DP

Oxford University Press is a department of the University of Oxford.
It furthers the University's objective of excellence in research, scholarship,
and education by publishing worldwide in

Oxford New York

Auckland Cape Town Dar es Salaam Hong Kong Karachi
Kuala Lumpur Madrid Melbourne Mexico City Nairobi
New Delhi Shanghai Taipei Toronto

With offices in

Argentina Austria Brazil Chile Czech Republic France Greece
Guatemala Hungary Italy Japan Poland Portugal Singapore
South Korea Switzerland Thailand Turkey Ukraine Vietnam

OXFORD and OXFORD ENGLISH are registered trade marks of
Oxford University Press in the UK and in certain other countries

ISBN-13: 978 0 19 437181 0
ISBN-10: 0 19 437181 6

Printed in China

Acknowledgements

We thank Paul Seligson for trying out some of the activities in this book and for his continued encouragement and support, Violeta Dobosz, from Poland, Laura Mazzaferro and her classes of 2001 at Nightingale School, San Isidro, Argentina for piloting many of the activities and for their feedback. Also, Pat Daponte of Wellspring School, Del Viso, Argentina for trying out the activities with her classes of 2002, Vicky Saumell, Claudia Rey, Oriel Villa Garcia and many more students and teachers who have tried out the materials in classes around the world especially in Coundon Court Comprehensive , Coventry, UK; Buena Vista School, Singapore; Manarat School, Riyadh, Saudia Arabia; and Aloha College, Marbella, Spain.

The authors and publisher are grateful to those who have given permission to reproduce the following extracts and adaptations of copyright material.

page 53 Media Awareness Network (2004) for 'Fish Out of Water'. Ottawa: MNet http://www.media-awareness.ca. Used with permission.

page 58 Extracts from *The Diary of a Teenage Health Freak* by Aidan Macfarlane and Ann McPherson (Oxford University Press, 2002), copyright © Aidan Macfarlane and Ann McPherson 1987, 1996, 2002. Reprinted by permission.

page 58 Extract from *True Confessions of Adrian Albert Mole* by Sue Townsend. Used by permission of The Random House Group Limited.

page 78 GDP from World Bank *World Development Report* 2000, cited in *Globalization* by Manfred B. Steger, Oxford University Press, 2003. Reprinted by permission.

page 83 Anti-GMO quote by Geraldene Holt. Reprinted by permission of Geraldene Holt.

page 83 Statement from Monsanto Co UK webpage www.monsanto.co.uk. Reprinted with permission.

page 88 Extract from 'Manifesto 2000 for a culture of Peace and non-violence' from www.unesco.org. Reprinted by permission of UNESCO.

page 90 Extract from 'I have a dream' by Martin Luther King. Reprinted by arrangement with the Estate of Martin Luther King Jr., c/o Writers House as agent for the proprietor, New York, NY. Copyright 1963 Martin Luther King Jr., copyright renewed 1991 Coretta Scott King.

page 92 'Behind the veil' by Vandna Synghal, *Orbit* 82, published by VSO, January 2002. Reprinted by permission of Orbit Magazine.

page 93 'What is a home?' edited by J. Monahan from *Changing Lives*, published by Crisis. Reprinted by permission of Crisis.

page 97 'Lebanon lights up' by Reem Haddad, *New Internationalist* Issue No. 332, March 2001. Reprinted by permission of *New Internationalist*.

page 100 'Exercise File: Linguistic diversity in the world' prepared by Josep Cru and Amélie Ponce from www.linguapax.org. Reprinted by permission of Linguapax Institute.

page 104 'Convention on the Rights of the Child' from www.unicef.org. Reprinted by permission of UNICEF.

page 107 'Child asylum seekers sold for sex' from http://news.bbc.co.uk, 8 March 2001. Reprinted by permission of BBC News Interactive.

page 131 'Who are we?' and p132 'We know' by Benjamin Zephaniah from the book *Wicked World* published by Puffin Books. Reprinted by permission of Benjamin Zephaniah.

page 115 'Everyone': words and music by Kristian Lundin & Andreas Carlsson © copyright 2000 Zomba Music Publishers Limited. All Rights Reserved. International copyright secured.

page 109 'Iron Hand': words and music by Mark Knopfler © copyright 1991 Rondor Music (London) Ltd. All Rights Reserved. International copyright secured.

page 121 'Another day in paradise': words and music by Phil Collins © 1989. Reproduced by permission of Philip Collins Ltd/Hit and Run Music (Publishing) Ltd, London WC2H 0QY

page 117 From 'Interview with Marilyn Manson', *NY Rock* September 2000. Reprinted by permission of NY Rock.

Sources

page 43 www.oneworld.org

page 65 'Coffee statistics' from *New Internationalist* A-Z of World Development CD-ROM 1999.

page 78 Sales from *Fortune*, July 31, 2000

Although every effort has been made to trace and contact copyright holders before publication, this has not been possible in some cases. We apologize for any apparent infringement of copyright and, if notified, the publisher will be pleased to rectify any errors or omissions at the earliest opportunity.

Illustrations by Mark Duffin: pages 20, 32, 33, 37, 53, 63.

Photos reproduced by permission of Alamy Images p. 102 (children in carpet factory/Mediacolors); Corbis p. 91 (Doctors at King Fahd Military Medical Complex/Jacques Langevin/Sygma); Lonely Planet images p. 53 (rock painting/John Hay)

Peters Map (p. 32) reproduced by permission of Oxford Cartographers.

Special thanks

From Susan:

Thanks to my close family: Mick, James, Sarah, Blanca, and Biscuit, the dog.

From Ricardo:

To my wife and life co-pilot Denise, to my son Esteban who makes my world go round, and to Hugo Bilsky, the master and friend.

Contents

Activity	Time (in minutes)	Aims	Page
3 Major Global Issues			75
3.1 Identify your rights	40	Reading for gist, making an oral summary; human rights, media literacy	75
3.2 Globalization	30	Speaking, writing; thinking about globalization; analysing a table, discussing pros and cons	77
3.3 AIDS today	40 in class + research time	Working with acronyms, writing, speaking; reflecting on AIDS	79
3.4 Questioning GMOs	15 for worksheet, 20 for reading and discussion, 40 for debate	Using persuasive language, arguments for and against; finding information about GMOs and discussing their risks and benefits	81
3.5 The death penalty	40 + follow-up	Speaking, holding a debate; discussing the death penalty	83
3.6 Our campaign against war	40 over several lessons, plus homework	Using tenses and modals, oral fluency; reflecting about the implications of war	85
3.7 The classroom for peace	40	Reading, oral discussion, imperatives; individual and group potential	87
3.8 Say no to racism	30 + design time	Reading comprehension, using imperatives; racism and ways to fight it	89
3.9 Behind the veil	60	Vocabulary related to advantages and disadvantages, discussion, presenting a case; stereotypes and prejudice	91
3.10 What is a home?	40	Vocabulary of houses and homes, *would* for likely outcome; homes and homelessness	93
3.11 Smoke screen	80	Using modals, discussion, giving presentations, reading; smoking issues	95
3.12 Endangered languages	40	Using imperatives, countries and languages; linguistic diversity	99
3.13 Child labour in focus	40 +	Expressions of frequency, adjectives to describe a picture; children's rights	102
3.14 Gender roles and you	40 plus survey time out of school hours	Present tense for everyday activities, arguing a case; gender role stereotypes	104
3.15 Human cargo	30 plus follow-up	Analysing a text, translation of issue-specific words; human trafficking	106

The authors and series editor

Ricardo Sampedro has taught English for various private language schools, given Ecology classes in a bilingual school in Buenos Aires, and also taught English in Spain at Euroschools. He worked for Oxford University Press Argentina for nearly ten years, giving hundreds of teacher training sessions and presentations for teachers of English all over Argentina, then served as ELT marketing manager until he left to launch an independent teacher training project on Global Issues called Education for a Change. Within this educational project he gives workshops and training courses dealing with issues such as environmental concerns, human rights, cultural understanding, education for peace, consumerism, and the mass media. The project's three main axes are the development of critical thinking skills, social skills, and empowerment.

He is currently a freelance speaker and teacher trainer based in Spain, where he is continuing his research into music and its implementation in the ELT classroom with special emphasis on Global Issues.

Susan Hillyard was awarded a Bachelor of Education in Educational Drama and Sociology from Warwick University in 1972. She has worked as a classroom teacher, co-ordinator, Head of Sector, teacher trainer, and speaker in the UK, Singapore, Saudi Arabia, Spain, and Argentina.

Until 2005 she was Secondary English Headmistress at Wellspring School, Argentina. She currently works as an Educational Consultant, delivering presentations on a variety of topics including creative teaching and learning, Global Issues, Drama in education, teaching thinking skills, and classroom management.

Alan Maley worked for The British Council from 1962 to 1988, serving as English Language Officer in Yugoslavia, Ghana, Italy, France, and China, and as Regional Representative in South India (Madras). From 1988 to 1993 he was Director-General of the Bell Educational Trust, Cambridge. From 1993 to 1998 he was Senior Fellow in the Department of English Language and Literature of the National University of Singapore, and from 1998 to 2003 he was Director of the graduate programme at Assumption University, Bangkok. He is currently a freelance consultant.

His publications include *Literature* (in this series), *Beyond Words, Sounds Interesting, Sounds Intriguing, Words, Variations on a Theme,* and *Drama Techniques in Language Learning* (all with Alan Duff), *The Mind's Eye* (with Françoise Grellet and Alan Duff), *Learning to Listen* and *Poem into Poem* (with Sandra Moulding), *Short and Sweet,* and *The English Teacher's Voice.*

Foreword

Global Issues can no longer be dismissed as something 'out there'. They are very much 'in here' too. We cannot escape them. They permeate every aspect of our lives: the food we eat, the water we drink, the air we breathe, the goods we buy, the holidays we take, the infections we contract ... The world is a web of intricately interdependent strands. Everything is touched by Global Issues. And in a global society obsessed with 'more' and 'faster', such issues are matters of human survival, not the concern of a minority of eccentric fringe groups. They can no longer be safely ignored.

It is legitimate to ask, however, why such issues should form part of the foreign language curriculum. At least four answers come to mind:

- Language teaching has no defined content. Global Issues are one area of concern which provides ready-made content.
- This content is not trivial, as is much of the contrived content of language coursebooks. It has obvious personal relevance for the lives of the learners.
- Global Issues expand the narrow scope of language learning to a wider educational perspective.
- The English language, as the principal vehicle of global consumerism (which lies at the heart of many, if not all, Global Issues), should bear some of the responsibility for making 'consumers' of English aware of some of its less desirable effects.

There are, of course, dangers in integrating Global Issues into language learning programmes. One is the risk of over-familiarity ('Oh no, not pollution again!'). A second is over-zealousness on the part of teachers. A crusading, evangelical stance towards Global Issues can deter rather than motivate learners. A third is that, in their enthusiasm for Global Issues, teachers may forget that the ultimate aim is also to teach language.

This book skilfully avoids these traps. It offers teachers a way of dealing with Global Issues in a responsible yet interesting way without trivialising them, while at the same time meeting learners' language learning needs. It helps learners to relate Global Issues to their own lives and experience, and offers ideas for them to act as well as to think.

In the words of Socrates, 'The unexamined life is not worth living'. And unless we examine it, there may well be no life left to examine.

Alan Maley

Introduction

Global Issues and English language teaching

Research among 11–16 year olds indicates that over 80 per cent are interested in Global Issues and feel they should learn about them at school (MORI 1998, for the Development Education Association). Social, economic, health, and environmental concerns, all Global Issues themselves, increasingly affect our lives. Every new 'natural' disaster that results from human activity, every new war waged, and every new globalization-related problem that condemns millions to a new dose of suffering and poverty impinges upon us.

There is increasing interest in Global Issues among the teaching community world-wide. Both of the major international English teachers' associations have established sections focusing on them: the IATEFL Global Issues Special Interest Group and the TESOL Social Responsibility Caucus. Local organizations such as the Japan Association of Language Teachers have also founded Global Issues interest groups. This points to a new direction in language teaching.

The primary aim of language teaching is to communicate with people from other cultures. It is a natural extension of this to challenge cultural and racial stereotypes, promote tolerance, and work to reduce conflict and inequality.

Language acquisition is meaningful only when it is viewed as part of the human condition. What we do as teachers and learners affects our own small ecosystems and beyond. This is why 'thinking globally and acting locally', or 'understanding and abiding by our human rights and responsibilities', should constitute a major guiding principle, not only in the classroom but also in our personal lives.

In a globalized world, where the effects of global financial and trade policies reach every corner of the planet, the need to understand other cultures and the interrelationships that bind us all together is increasingly important. To this end we have used a variety of techniques to tackle stereotypes and cultural barriers.

This book offers a wide range of activities, dealing with many Global Issues. It focuses on the development of critical thinking to encourage a questioning attitude on the part of students. The many opportunities offered for meaningful debate, discussion, reasoning, and expressing different points of view, help to develop and improve communication skills.

The aim of the book is twofold:

- To provide easy-to-use classroom activities to enliven and enrich English language classes, while at the same time promoting a fresh and questioning approach to global and social issues.
- *Global Issues* regards language teaching as closely related to the global life we live. Given that language and thought are directly related, this book views language as a natural vehicle for fostering cross-cultural, cross-boundary understanding and for raising awareness on global and social issues.

The issues covered include: discrimination, equal opportunities, racism, human rights, globalization, health, the impact of the media, consumer education, environmental concerns, conflict and peace, poverty, the use and misuse of natural resources, fair trade, indigenous knowledge, the arms trade, genetically modified organisms, homelessness, disappearing languages, social justice, perceptions and stereotypes, sustainability, and refugees, among others.

We have chosen to focus on issues which we feel are likely to maintain or even increase their relevance. However, as world events and circumstances change over time, some issues will grow or reduce in importance, and some will be more significant in certain contexts than in others. In most cases the techniques are adaptable to other topics, and we encourage teachers and students to exercise their critical thinking skills, and to experiment and adapt.

Interactive teaching and learning

Inherent within the philosophy of this book is the idea that the teaching and learning process must be interactive; it must be learner-centred; it must be about human relationships; it must be about the dual process, the to-ing and fro-ing of the teaching and learning situation. A book about Global Issues could not possibly ignore this ideal. We feel we need to promote, firstly, within the classroom itself, such values as tolerance, empathy, sharing, turn-taking, and creative and critical thinking skills.

Techniques used include individual 'think time' (see below), pair work for discussion or improvisation, group work for brainstorming and research, whole-class discussion and data collection, surveys, interviews, games, drama, poetry appreciation, and writing exercises. In group work we make use of scribes and speakers appointed by groups, and we encourage discussion and debate. Much depends on the teacher's ability to facilitate these activities and if they are new to you, you may experience some teething troubles. However, with conviction and persistence you will find that this kind of work can motivate students to work together and with you, the teacher, and to become proactive individuals using information and thinking skills to question local and world issues. It will also help your students to develop their own identities and to develop and express reasoned opinions.

Developing critical thinking

The way we view the world and relate to others is intrinsically connected to our own set of values, and it is these values that govern the way we decide to live. However, the influence of fashion, consumerism, pop culture, broken homes, social unrest, and the media is all-pervasive. For many people, teachers and students alike, this influence goes unquestioned. Critical thinking, if successfully taught at this level, becomes the antidote for individual and social illiteracy. For the authors, critical thinking should constitute an indivisible part of the overall educational process. Facione (1995) comments: 'Critical thinking lies at the root of civilisation. It is a cornerstone in the journey humankind is taking from beastly savagery to global sensitivity'.

By critical thinking we mean the basic skills of:
- analysis
- inference
- explanation
- interpretation
- evaluation
- self-regulation.

In addition, teachers need to encourage students to develop qualities which contribute to critical thinking, such as:
- open-mindedness
- inquisitiveness
- good judgement
- truth-seeking
- confidence in their own powers of reasoning and expression
- being systematic.

Supporting the development of these skills involves reflective teaching and learning, which is highly complex and which some students may find difficult, or interpret as weakness on the part of teacher. But in the long run, with patience on the part of the teacher, it will develop students who can view old or new material, from a variety of sources, through new eyes, using their skills to define their own stance and express it, often better in their second language, with an open-minded confidence.

Developing creative thinking

Having stressed critical thinking, we are also aware of the need to combine this with creativity. After all, Einstein is quoted as saying

'Imagination is more important than knowledge. For knowledge is limited, whereas imagination embraces the entire world'. We are also aware that, as we mention in Chapter 4, 'Music, drama, and communication skills', many students need to work through other channels of expression when learning a foreign language. We agree with Dilts and Epstein (1991) that creativity requires all three facets of the person who can:

- dream
- plan and act
- criticize the product and the self.

In developing these dispositions through the four main areas of fluency, flexibility, originality and elaboration (Fisher 1995), we stress the importance of combining cognitive skills with affective aspects to perform, produce, or publish.

Many of the activities in this book include language arts processes such as language skills, art, music, drama, and games, as well as reflection and self-evaluation.

Think time

'Think time' is an indispensable tool for teaching reflective learning which promotes student autonomy and plays a major role in 'learning to learn'. We thank Merrill Swain for suggesting this idea and for helping us to develop it into a simple, efficient device for helping students to use their thinking skills in a concrete and fairly painless manner.

It is essential to teach your students to think about issues on their own, with their own thoughts, in their own way *before* they combine ideas and discuss them in groups, with you, or as a whole class. Here are a few basic rules to increase the effectiveness of the technique:

1 Ask one or more open-ended questions.
2 Give a specified amount of *silent* think time (this means *nobody*, including you, the teacher, may speak—this is the hardest part). Often it will only last 2–3 minutes but it must be done in total silence.
3 Everybody should write notes on their thoughts. There are no right or wrong answers. Everything is useful and important.
4 Allow time for each student to read back their own answers silently to themselves.
5 Allow time to readjust or add to their answers if they want.

An important feature of 'Think time', besides the reasons given above relating to thinking and evaluating one's own thoughts, is that it is a quick integrated language lesson all on its own. The students listen, write, read (back to themselves), and speak (to themselves, initially), all in a few minutes.

Student research

With all the means now available it is now relatively easier to have students doing their own research, but we must give them time and teach them methods for conducting research. It should not be assumed that students know how to do this, even in their mother tongue. It is essential that the teacher genuinely *teaches* learning to learn.

Thinking skills must be applied to all information gathered. Students should be taught to:
- plan
- search
- skim and scan
- read and comprehend
- sift and select
- make connections
- evaluate
- summarize in their own way using their own expressions
- apply
- present.

Much depends on the resources available. Some institutions have sophisticated libraries, computer laboratories, or resource centres manned by experts who are available full-time to help students. Other places have very little in the way of resources and the teacher is left to his/her own devices to supply materials. In many cases, the success of an activity is dependent on the accessibility of information, which can be designed by the teacher, photocopied from the photocopiable materials provided in the book, or researched and shared by the students, their parents, friends, colleagues, and local agencies. However, by no means all the activities require information from outside sources.

It is preferable to work with materials produced in the English language, but it is not always essential. References have been suggested for most of the activities in the book, and the Internet is a useful, up-to-date resource if you have access. Further information on teaching resources is provided in the Reference Library. We recommend that you use up-to-date sources as the situation regarding many Global Issues can change rapidly.

In every case, it will be the teacher's job to decide beforehand what is feasible. We therefore leave that to your own judgement, within your own context.

This book does not constitute a programme to be followed to the letter but is instead intended as a teaching tool. In many cases you can use the activities as they are, but you can also use them as a springboard for further investigation and innovation. You will need to take into account your own geographical, social, educational, and political context in order to judge which activities are suitable for your classes, and whether it is necessary to adapt them. We have deliberately avoided indicating when an activity is suitable for different contexts, as nobody is in a better position to judge this than the teacher in his or her own teaching context.

Of course this is not the only way to approach teaching using Global Issues. The ideas and activities contained in this book are tried and tested and have worked for us, but the success of an activity depends, as we all know, on a multitude of internal and external factors. We hope that the ideas in this book will inspire teachers to develop their own learning activities with a social slant, to suit their own teaching situations.

How this book is organized

The activities in this book are arranged into chapters which are intended to help teachers to introduce and develop Global Issues in the classroom.

Chapter 1, 'Awareness raising', develops awareness of a number of important Global Issues by encouraging students to look at items they use in their everyday lives in a new light, or by adapting traditional games and classroom activities.

Chapter 2, 'Personal experiences', makes use of students' prior knowledge of the world and their personal experiences to help them reflect on how everyday events and situations can be related to Global Issues.

Chapter 3, 'Major Global Issues', demonstrates activities which can be used to focus on particular issues. We have chosen topics which we feel are likely to remain relevant; however, in most cases the procedures are adaptable to other topics of interest to your students.

Chapter 4, 'Music, drama, and communication skills in Global Issues', looks at ways to use techniques such as drama, music, poetry, choral speaking, presentations, and projects such as making a newscast, to explore Global Issues.

The Reference Library contains guidance on finding further information and is organized by material type. Within each section the suggestions are arranged by topic. The types of resources included are:

- Useful background reading and books referred to in the text (bibliography)
- Educational packs and other teaching resources
- Websites featuring teaching ideas. There is a huge number of websites on particular issues, so we have concentrated on those which offer useful teaching ideas and materials. The Internet is constantly changing, but the web addresses given were correct at the time of going to press. Inclusion in these lists does not necessarily mean that the authors or publishers of this book endorse these sites or their content.
- Non-governmental organizations which campaign on particular issues
- Government-related agencies such as the United Nations and the World Health Organization.

The Glossary provides definitions of key specialist terms used in the discussion of various issues, to help you explain them to your students. Terms explained in the Glossary are **highlighted** in the text.

The Index helps you find activities quickly on particular topics and language points.

The majority of the book consists of lesson plans and classroom activities, which all follow a similar format to make it easy to choose an activity to suit your students.

Level

This may vary according to the adaptations you can make. Usually it indicates the minimum level that the activity is recommended for, although this will vary in different contexts, and of course you know your students best. There are often Variations which suggest ways of adapting the activity for other levels.

Time

The time given is a suggestion for guidance and may vary with different classes. Often suggestions are made for splitting up longer activities over two or more lessons.

Aims

The language aims show the language point(s) that the activity was designed to practise, although of course this may change if you decide to use different materials or topics. We view Global Issues and language teaching as an indivisible part of the overall educational process: the 'other' aims refer to non-linguistic skills which are also practised.

Materials

Anything you need to have available in order to do the activity.

Background information box

This provides some facts and data on the particular issue referred to.

Word store

Useful vocabulary which students may need for this activity.

Preparation

Anything you may need to do before the lesson.

Procedure

This shows, in clear numbered steps, how to set up and carry out the activity.

Variations

These include ideas on how to adapt the activity to suit different levels, alternative topics, or other ways of delivering the activity.

Follow-ups

Optional extra activities which give students opportunities to look at the issues in greater depth.

Recommended resources

Resources you may find useful to provide more information on the issue in question, or suggestions for films and songs which can help to bring the issue to life for students. More details are provided in the Reference Library.

Website

For extra activites, downloadable worksheets, web links, and more information visit the Resource Books for Teachers website www.oup.com/elt/teacher/rbt.

1

Awareness raising

Global Issues increasingly affect our everyday lives, regardless of our geographical location. It is also unquestionable that in some regions problems such as war, conflict, hunger, and poverty are extremely close to home. Global news coverage has brought many of these issues into the spotlight, and teenagers are gradually becoming more aware of social and environmental issues. Their favourite actors and music and sports stars not only express their views on relevant world issues but raise awareness. Awareness raising is of great importance in the educational context, and the ELT classroom is no exception.

With this aim in mind we have included in this chapter activities which, through a range of techniques, develop awareness of a number of relevant Global Issues. Some of the activities, such as 1.8, 'Global bingo', page 28, or 1.9, 'Global drains and ladders', page 31, are variations on traditional games with a Global Issues slant. Others make use of authentic materials, for example, newspapers as in 1.6, 'Looking for headlines', page 24. Other activities encourage students to analyse everyday items such as product labels in a critical light (1.7, 'Reading the labels', page 26). In addition, this chapter features a 'Global quiz' (1.14, page 42), in which statements by prominent people are used as springboards for discussion and research, while in other activities issues such as smoking are approached from an individual and group perspective to promote general debate (see 1.10, 'Clouds of smoke', page 34). The common thread permeating all these activities is to develop critical thinking and social skills.

1.1 Your footprint on the Earth

Humanity's current impact on the planet far exceeds the Earth's capacity. In this activity, students reflect on the impact of various daily activities, and think of ways of reducing their 'footprint on the Earth'.

Level	Lower-intermediate and above
Time	40 minutes
Aims	LANGUAGE Using modals and gerunds. OTHER Understanding our individual impact on Earth.
Materials	One copy of the worksheet for each student.

Word store

footprint   impact   **genetically modified organisms (GMOs)**
packaging   free-range   **recycling**   to insulate   in bulk
waste   to re-use   organic food   processed food
battery farming   **sustainability**

Procedure

1 Explain the concept of 'our footprint on the Earth': the impact that our activities have on the planet in terms of resources used. Ask the students for a few examples of how we can reduce this impact, for example, travelling by train instead of by car, or recycling bottles rather than throwing them away.

2 Explain that there are different ways to measure this 'footprint' and that they are going to assess their own impact on the Earth in four major categories: transport, food, waste, and energy.

3 Give each student a copy of the worksheet.

Worksheet 1.1.
Your footprint on the Earth

Transport	
OK	Heavy impact

Food	
OK	Heavy impact

Waste	
OK	Heavy impact

Energy	
OK	Heavy impact

Photocopiable © Oxford University Press

4   Ask them to think for a moment about these four categories and how they relate to their everyday lives—the kind of food they eat, how they travel to school or other places, what they do with the waste they generate, what energy resources they use unnecessarily, etc. For further ideas you can refer to the Prompt box below (for example, 'biking to school' helps reduce our impact on the Earth while 'using a car' has a heavier impact).

5   Ask them to write their daily activities in each of the four categories in either the 'OK' or the 'Heavy impact' column, according to how much of an impact they feel the activities have on the planet (for example, turning off the lights when nobody is in the room should go under 'OK' while 'leaving the lights on' should go in the 'Heavy impact' column).

6   Ask them to discuss their results in pairs and to try to list a few ideas on how to reduce their 'footprint on the planet'.

7   Ask the students for suggestions and make notes on the board.

8   Ask the students to put these into grammatically correct sentences. You could ask them to use modals, passives, and expressions or vocabulary they have learnt, such as *To reduce my impact on Earth I* **should** *bike to school instead of* **being driven** *there by my Dad or Mum.*

Prompt box

Transport

How do I go to school? (by bike/motorbike/bus/car/other)
What method of transport do I regularly use?

Food

Do I eat a lot of products of animal origin? Do I eat a lot of vegetables? Do I eat organic food? Do I eat locally produced fruit or (exotic) fruits grown on the other side of the world? Do I eat free-range or battery eggs? Do I eat a lot of processed food?

Waste

Do I buy things in bulk? Do I buy things with a lot of packaging? What do I do with the waste I generate (organic, paper, plastics, cans, etc.)? Do I re-use things? Do I throw away many re-usable things? Do I recycle on a regular basis?

Energy

Are the home appliances and light bulbs I use energy-efficient? Is my home insulated? Do I turn off the lights and other appliances when I don't need them (such as the television, the radio, etc.)? Do I turn down the heating at home?

Follow-up

Ask the students to write a report or prepare a poster identifying activities that help reduce human impact on the planet. They can refer to websites, encyclopaedias, and other reference materials. Give them a few days to gather the information. (Set a clear deadline!)

Recommended resources

The Ecological Footprint Quiz, produced by Redefining Progress and the Earth Day Network.

1001 Ways to Save the Planet by Bernadette Vallely.

Recycling by Rosemary Border, Oxford University Press.

The Next Step: 50 More Things you Can Do to Save the Earth, published by the Earth Works Group.

1.2 Telling films

Telling films asks questions about how war films portray the sides involved, and give or omit relevant information. The activity activates students' critical thinking skills and encourages them to look for information on world events associated with the conflict shown, and to spot political bias.

Level Lower-intermediate and above

Time 40 minutes plus viewing time

Aims LANGUAGE Use of simple present and simple past. Names of countries. Expressing opinions.
        OTHER   Media literacy, identifying bias in films.

Materials One copy of the question sheet for each group of three students.

Procedure

1 Ask the class to think of all the war films they have seen and to try to remember their names.

2 List these on the board.

3 Elicit which countries were involved in the conflict in each film and write these next to the name of the film.

4 Put the students into groups of three (it is preferable if they have seen the same films), and give each group a copy of the question sheet. Ask them to discuss the answers and jot down their responses. You may need to explain vocabulary such as 'humane' and 'suffer'.

5 Elicit the groups' responses.

6 Conduct a whole class discussion, focusing on the following questions:
a Are war films made for entertainment only?
b Who benefits from the messages conveyed?

War films

a Write down the names of the films and the countries fighting in them. Which of the two sides in each film is shown as more humane? Put an H next to that country's name.

b Which side appears to suffer more? Put an S next to that country's name. If there is any evidence in the film to support this, give examples.

c How do the films show the feelings of both sides?

d Is the viewer informed as to why the war was being fought? When?

e Explain why that war—if it really happened—took place.

f Are the sides depicted as 'goodies' and 'baddies'? If so, who are the 'goodies' in these films?

Variation 1

You could show selected sequences from several films in order to
- provide content
- prompt reactions.

Variation 2

Films on other topics could be discussed in the same way, for example, relations between the sexes or between generations.

Recommended resources

Film, Resource Books for Teachers series, Oxford University Press.

Mixed Media section on the New Internationalist website.

1.3 The global citizen

This activity encourages students first to reflect on our rights and responsibilities with regard to the different types of communities to which we belong, and then to discuss the meaning of 'global community'.

Level   Elementary and above

Time   20 minutes

Aims   LANGUAGE   Using modals. Making suggestions.

OTHER   To raise awareness on and to instil a sense of belonging to the global community.

Procedure

1   Put the students into groups of three or four.

2 Explain that we all have a role as members of the community we live in. For example, within the family we have a defined role as sons, daughters, or parents; at school, teachers have a defined role while students have another.

3 Also explain that each of those roles is 'supported' by a number of duties, responsibilities, and rights.

4 Draw a mid-sized circle on the board and write 'family' within it. Explain that this is the smallest and first community we all belong to.

5 Draw a second circle around the first, and then several others until you have a good number of circles, one inside the other.

6 Ask the students to copy the circles. In their groups, they should discuss what communities are represented by the circles (for example, school, nation, tribe, group of friends, city). They write this within each circle.

7 Ask them to define what they think their duties, rights, and responsibilities are as members of each of those communities. Ask them to write these next to each circle.

8 The groups take turns to share their results with the class. Encourage contributions from other groups.

9 Now draw a large circle around all the circles on the board and write on top 'global community'.

10 Elicit the students' ideas on the following questions:

11 In their groups, the students make a list of principles they think should govern our global community.

12 Conduct a full-class discussion.

Follow-up

Students research and prepare a poster on Global Citizenship projects currently being developed around the world, focusing on how students from different countries can participate in these projects.

Global community

a What does it mean to be a member of the global community?

b What is the relationship between our global community responsibilities and, for example, the pollution of the world's rivers, the greenhouse effect, and the destruction of the rainforests?

c What are your responsibilities towards other members of the global community?

Photocopiable © Oxford University Press

Recommended resources

A Citizenship for the Future, published by WWF.

A Curriculum for Global Citizenship, published by OXFAM.

Charter 99 website.

Jubilee 2000 Coalition website.

World Social Forum website.

Agenda 21 on the United Nations website (UN Conference on Environment and Development).

The Earth Charter on The Earth Charter Initiative website.

1.4 Quick spin around the world

This activity explores our ideas on 'national characteristics' and challenges prejudice and stereotypes.

Level Elementary and above

Time 25 minutes

Aims LANGUAGE Proper names of countries, nationalities, and associated objects.

OTHER To show that stereotypes and prejudice do not hold true and to help understand that there is a lot more to other countries than symbols or stereotypes.

Materials One encyclopaedia or other reference material per group, and/or Internet access.

Procedure

1 Copy on to the board, or display, a large colourful alphabet.

2 Divide the alphabet into groups of letters: for example, A, B, C, D, and E; F, G, H, I, and J, etc.) but leave the Z out. This letter can be used by any group to replace another.

3 Arrange the class into five groups and give each a group of letters.

4 Ask the groups to think of names of countries starting with each of the five letters they have. If they cannot think of one, they can use Z instead of that letter.

Example A–Argentina, B–Britain, C–Canada, D–Denmark, E–Egypt

5 Ask them to brainstorm and to identify a thing or person which they feel represents each of the countries they have listed.

Example Argentina–Maradona, Britain–Big Ben, Canada–Mounties, Denmark–bacon, Egypt–the pyramids

6 Write the names of the countries and objects on the board by the alphabet letters.

7 Elicit adjectives which the students feel could go well with the different countries (for example, *poor, developed, rich, cold, arrogant, exotic*).

8 Ask if any students have travelled to any of the countries and, if so, ask them to share their experiences.

9 Put the class into small groups.

10 Ask each group to choose any one country. With the aid of the reference materials, they prepare a brief fact file on that country with information they feel is important.

11 For homework, ask each group to focus on the next group of letters, so that the group that had A, B, C, D, and E will now work on F, G, H, I, and J, and so on. Ask them to select one of the countries in their new letter group and to find out about:
- history
- development status
- culture
- sport
- scientific achievements.

Follow-up

Students can do some more thorough research into the selected countries and prepare a fact file.

Recommended resources

Social Indicators table on the United Nations website.

Country Profiles on the CARE website.

Country Profiles on the New Internationalist website.

The State of the World published by the WorldWatch Institute.

1.5 Positive and negative

Through group and class discussions, students reflect on what causes anti-social behaviour and what can be done to improve it.

Level Lower-intermediate and above

Time 40 minutes

Aims LANGUAGE Using gerunds and *should* for advice.
OTHER To reflect on the way we relate to the place we live in and to other people.

Word store

anti-social behaviour   litter   public property

vandalism/to vandalize   to take care   to be rude/polite

to assist   public nuisance

Procedure

1 Divide the board vertically into two sections and write POSITIVE on one side and NEGATIVE on the other.

2 Elicit from the class what are the good (positive) things we can do in our daily living environments (for example, school, work, home, street, or club) which are also good for other people. Write them up on the board under POSITIVE.

Examples Saying hello, helping blind people across the street, giving directions to strangers, putting rubbish in litter bins, protecting our natural environment, helping people in need (homeless people, elderly people, physically challenged people), being kind, etc.

3 Do the same with the bad (NEGATIVE) things we can do which affect other people. Write them up on the board under NEGATIVE.

Examples Vandalizing public property, dropping litter, jumping the lights, jumping the queue, not cleaning up your pet's droppings, being rude, bullying, being selfish, gossiping about other people, etc.

4 Arrange the class into groups of three and ask the students to brainstorm on why people do the things listed under POSITIVE.

5 Ask the groups to write their ideas in note form.

6 Do the same with the things listed under NEGATIVE.

7 Hold a general discussion on/about each of the things listed under NEGATIVE.

8 Elicit ideas to improve the things/situations listed under NEGATIVE.

Follow-up

Discuss how we behave towards other people and the places where we live. Students could write an essay or produce a poster for homework.

1.6 Looking for headlines

This activity helps students identify Global Issues related to daily events while at the same time promoting critical thinking in relation to newspapers and news in general.

Level   Intermediate and above

Time   40 minutes

Aims   LANGUAGE   Reading for gist
   OTHER   Raising awareness of global issues addressed in local newspapers

Materials   Copies of newspapers collected over a week.

Word store

issue   article   cutting

front page   headline   news   relevance

Preparation

Tell the students to collect newspapers from home (or a neighbour, friend, or relative) for a week. If you live in a non-English speaking country, local newspapers can be used anyway as all the activity stages are developed in English.

Procedure

1 Collect all the newspapers together, put the students into pairs, and give out several newspapers per pair.

2 Elicit from the class the definition of 'Global Issue'. Help out by suggesting that these could be things/events which are global in scope (= crossing national boundaries). Give a few examples of local news stories such as crime, drugs, traffic and pollution problems, or homeless people, which might have global relevance. Elicit more examples and write some on the board.

3 Ask the students to sort their newspapers by date, and to find front-page articles which address Global Issues. From these they will select those they think are more important. Write up on the board the following guiding questions:
   a What is the global issue addressed?
   b Does the issue have international, national, or local consequences? Who or what will be affected?
   The students can write their findings on a worksheet such as the one below.

4 Ask the students to share their results with another pair, to try to find similarities and differences in their selection of articles, and to justify their choice.

5 Draw a large worksheet on the board appoint an assistant, and elicit results from the class so as to collate all the information together.

6 Ask the class to analyse the final results. The following questions may
be of help:

 a Did different newspapers give the same importance to the same
 issues?
 b Did you agree on what were the global issues addressed in the
 articles?
 c Are there any issues which are featured more than once? If so,
 which ones?
 d Do any of the articles deal with something that has personal
 implications for you?

Worksheet Names of students:				
Date	Newspaper	Article Title	Global Issue	Comments

Photocopiable © Oxford University Press

Variation

Students could work with television or radio news items instead of
newspapers.

Recommended resources

We the Media, published by The New Press

Newspapers, Oxford University Press (Resource Books for Teachers)

'Teachable moments' section of the Media Awareness website

Awareness raising | 25

1.7 Reading the labels

In this activity students are invited to take a closer look at the information on the labels of products they often consume.

Level Intermediate and above.

Time 40 minutes

Aims LANGUAGE Vocabulary of measurement systems. Vocabulary found on food labels.

OTHER Raising awareness of available information which is often unread.

Materials Empty containers, bottles, labels, etc. brought in by the students. At least two different coloured pens for each student.

Word store

consume/consumer   item   product   convenience food
ready meals   manufacturer/to manufacture   factual
non-factual   origin   ingredient   symbols
measurement systems   additives   **fair trade**   free-range
label/to label   organic   pesticide-free   flavourings
preservatives   free from
genetically modified organisms (GMOs)   processed
cruelty-free

Preparation

1 Ask the students to collect containers or labels from products they regularly consume, such as yoghurt, jam, juice, soft drink bottles and cans, cereal boxes, ready meals, etc. Ask them to do this for at least a week so there are plenty of items. They should wash the containers before bringing them to school.

2 Photocopy the worksheet and Label Analysis Sheet below.

Procedure

1 Put all items out on a convenient and accessible surface. Arrange the class into groups and give several items to each group. Tell them to select two and return the rest to the general pile, so that they have space to work.

2 Take them through the worksheet.

3 Walk around the class helping out with difficult words or concepts. Ask them to convert measurement systems if they are learning US English.

4 Write on the board the outline of the *Label Analysis Sheet* and ask students to copy it on their individual pieces of paper, or photocopy one for each student.

Worksheet 1.7

a If the labels are not in English, write the details first in the original language, and then find the English equivalents. Write it next to the original information, preferably in a different colour. For example:

Grapefruit juice carton

My language	In English
Quantity = litros (1 litro)	Fluid Ounces (36 fl oz)
Origin = Entre Ríos, Argentina	
Ingredients = agua mineral,	mineral water,
jugo de pomelo concentrado, etc.	concentrated grapefruit juice, etc.

b Was all or part of the information in more than one language? If so, which one/s? What do you think is the reason for this?

c Copy out the information on the labels that you found most important.

d Copy out any claims (non-factual information) on the labels that are difficult to verify (for example, 'this is the best mineral water you can drink'). Why do companies include this type of information? Is it fair?

5 Elicit results from the groups, encouraging comments and contributions from the whole class.

6 Ask them to write up their findings individually on their own Label Analysis Sheet.

7 Round off by asking the students what they think they have learnt from this activity.

Label analysis sheet

Product	Type of container
Factual information (information that can be checked, such as contents, ingredients, etc.):	**Other information**

Recommended resources

The Earth Journal—Environmental Almanac and Resource Directory, published by Buzzworm Books.

Friends of the Earth magazine or website.

The Ethical Consumer website.

1.8 Global bingo

A variation of the game *Bingo* using concepts and issues related to students' knowledge about Global Issues.

Level Upper-intermediate and above

Time 40 minutes

Aims LANGUAGE Matching definitions with words. Expressing opinions.

OTHER Reinforcing conceptual information by matching definitions and words.

Materials Copies of the photocopiable Global bingo cards.

Word store

human rights **racism** **discrimination** **natural resources**
advertising adverts **ozone layer** **greenhouse effect**
overconsumption recycling **indigenous peoples**
biodiversity rainforest

Preparation

1 Make enough copies of the photocopiable Global bingo cards for each student to have one card.

2 Pre-teach vocabulary where necessary.

Procedure

1 Explain to the class that they are going to play a kind of bingo. Explain the rules: you will read out sentences which students have to match with the concepts on their cards.

2 Give each student a Global bingo card.

3 Read out each Global bingo sentence twice, giving the numbers.

4 As you read, the students scan their cards for words or concepts that match the definitions you read. Tell them to write the sentence number next to the matching words/concepts.

5 The first student to match four terms on his or her card should raise his or her hand and shout 'Global bingo!' You then stop the game and ask that student for his or her results. Check that they are correct. If they are not, continue the game. (Note that not all the concepts on the cards are included in the sentences.)

6 Answer questions and clarify any confusing concepts.

7 After all the Global bingo matches have been checked out loud, and students have had time to correct any mistakes, arrange the class into groups of three and ask them to brainstorm one of the issues on the cards.

8 After five minutes, regroup the students into different threes, and ask them to select a new issue and brainstorm again.

9 Ask the students to share with the rest of the class points of agreement or disagreement from their discussions, or anything they want to say about the issues.

Follow-up

Repeat the game if you have time.

Global bingo sentences

1 Collecting items and reprocessing the materials so that they can be used again is called …
Answer: recycling

2 Regularly buying lots of things you do not need is known as …
Answer: overconsumption

3 The layer of gases that protect the earth from ultraviolet radiation is called …
Answer: the ozone layer

4 Amnesty International is an organization working for …
Answer: human rights

5 This means judging others by their skin colour, religion, or place of origin.
Answer: racism

6 Many developed nations depend on this resource, and wars are fought over it.
Answer: oil

7 The original inhabitants of a country or region are called …
Answer: indigenous peoples

8 This resource is polluted in many parts of the world and yet, clean _____ is essential to life.
Answer: water

9 People without a place to live are …
Answer: homeless

10 This can provide a huge amount of information, allows people in different parts of the world to communicate very fast, and is great fun, but it cannot replace formal education.
Answer: the Internet

11 The main goal of this is to create in us the need to acquire something specific.
Answer: advertising

Variation

You can alter the language level by making your own cards and sentences. You can also adapt the topics to your own syllabus or your students' interests.

Global bingo cards

Ozone layer
Homeless
Fair Trade
Overconsumption
Greenhouse Effect
Recycling
Discrimination
	Biodiversity
	Racism
	Human rights
	Oil
	Genetically Modified
	    Organisms (GMOs)
	Water
	Advertising
		The Internet
		Recycling
		Advertising
		Indigenous Peoples
		Transnational
		    Corporations (TNCs)
		Education
		Sweatshops

Ozone layer
Homeless
Fair Trade
Overconsumption
Greenhouse Effect
Recycling
Discrimination
	Biodiversity
	Racism
	Human rights
	Oil
	Genetically Modified
	    Organisms (GMOs)
	Water
	Advertising
		The Internet
		Recycling
		Advertising
		Indigenous Peoples
		Transnational
		    Corporations (TNCs)
		Education
		Sweatshops

Ozone layer
Homeless
Fair Trade
Overconsumption
Greenhouse Effect
Recycling
Discrimination
	Biodiversity
	Racism
	Human rights
	Oil
	Genetically Modified
	    Organisms (GMOs)
	Water
	Advertising
		The Internet
		Recycling
		Advertising
		Indigenous Peoples
		Transnational
		    Corporations (TNCs)
		Education
		Sweatshops

Photocopiable © Oxford University Press

1.9 Global drains and ladders

This game is a 'globalized' version of the traditional *Snakes and ladders*, in which players must get to the final square to win. On the way, they land on squares which can propel them forward (ladders) if they answer the question correctly, or on squares that can throw them *down the drain* if they fail to respond correctly.

Level Intermediate and above

Time 40 minutes

Aims LANGUAGE Reading questions and answering verbally.
OTHER Knowledge and accurate expression of some Global Issues.

Materials One set of question cards per group of three or four, one game board per group of three or four, one die per group, one coin or coloured token per student, one Peters Projection world map (see the Reference Library).

Procedure

1 Put the students into threes or fours and give each group a board, a die, three or four tokens and a set of question cards.

2 Tell them to put the question cards into piles of 'drains' and 'ladders' face up next to the board, with the cover card on top.

3 Explain that if they 'go down the drain' they are likely to lose, whereas going up a ladder can help them win.

4 Tell the students they should play the game, throwing the die in turns. The aim is to reach the end (square 49) but if they land on a square with a ladder or a drain, they must pick up the corresponding card and answer the question on it. The answers are on the back so they must not look at them beforehand!

5 There are two types of question cards. If the students fail to answer a *drain question*, they must go back (or down) the number of squares indicated but if they answer correctly, they stay where they are. If they answer a *ladder question* correctly, they move up to the end of that ladder, but if they get it wrong, they stay where they are for that round.

6 The cards cannot be used a second time.

7 When you have a winner, elicit responses to the questions and ask the students to locate the geographical areas or countries on the world map.

Peters projection world map

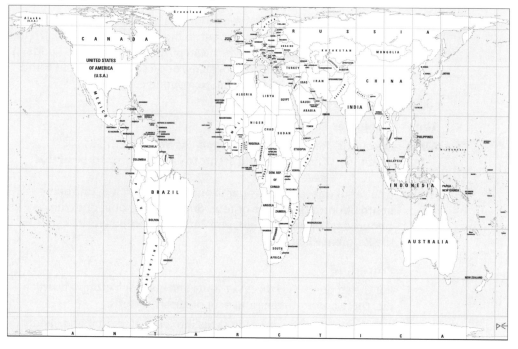

Global Drains and Ladders board

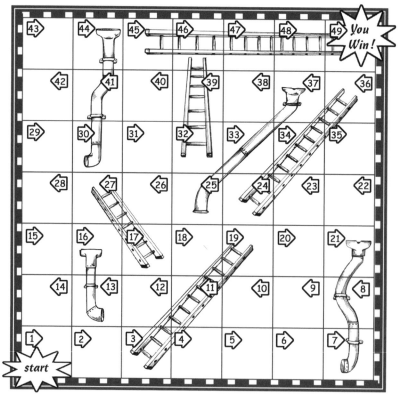

Photocopiable © Oxford University Press

Question cards

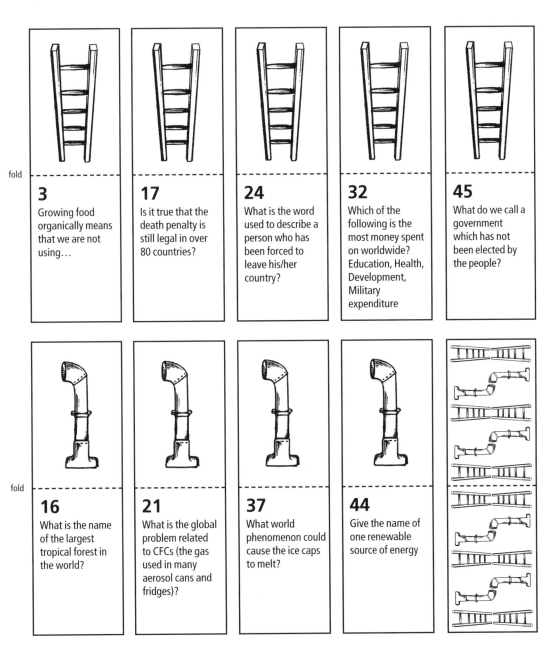

fold

3
Growing food organically means that we are not using…

17
Is it true that the death penalty is still legal in over 80 countries?

24
What is the word used to describe a person who has been forced to leave his/her country?

32
Which of the following is the most money spent on worldwide? Education, Health, Development, Military expenditure

45
What do we call a government which has not been elected by the people?

fold

16
What is the name of the largest tropical forest in the world?

21
What is the global problem related to CFCs (the gas used in many aerosol cans and fridges)?

37
What world phenomenon could cause the ice caps to melt?

44
Give the name of one renewable source of energy

Answers

3 Chemical pesticides
16 The Amazon
17 Yes

21 The hole in the ozone layer
24 Refugee
32 Military expenditure

37 Global warming
44 The sun, the wind, waves, tides
45 Dictatorship

1.10 Clouds of smoke

In this activity students are invited to think on their own, then to brainstorm in groups, and finally to discuss the rights of both non-smokers and smokers and to reach a general conclusion on the risks associated with smoking.

Level Intermediate and above

Time 40 minutes

Aims LANGUAGE Expressing likes and dislikes, negotiating, reaching consensus.

OTHER Accepting other people's ideas and views, raising awareness of the dangers associated with smoking.

Word store

passive smoking   World Health Organization   cancer

health risks   air **pollution**   **rights**   compromise   non-smoker

smoker

Procedure

1 Ask students to take two minutes' silent time, thinking on their own, and making notes on the questions:

a Do you smoke? If yes, how long have you smoked for? Why did you start? Do you enjoy smoking? Do you resent the 'no smoking' signs you see?

b If you don't smoke, how do you feel when other people light up in the same room as you are in? Have you ever felt under pressure to smoke?

2 Ask the smokers in the class to put up their hands, then do the same with non-smokers and calculate roughly the proportion of smokers compared to non-smokers.

- Are the majority of students smokers or non-smokers?
- Why is that?
- Does the proportion bear any relation to gender?

3 Divide the class into smokers and non-smokers and then divide each of the groups into smaller groups (ideally 4–6) so that you have several groups of non-smokers and smokers.

4 Write the phrases below on the board and ask the groups to brainstorm and write down a few ideas. Here are a few discussion starters:

Non-smoker groups

a their right to breathe clean air

b the health hazards of smoking

c passive smoking

Smoker groups

a their right to smoke when and where they want
b their right not to be discriminated against
Then get the groups to discuss their ideas.

5 Split each group in half and pair it with an 'opposing' group (i.e. smokers sit with non-smokers). Each group should appoint a scribe and a speaker. Tell them to share their conclusions and then discuss the issues again, with each side expressing their feelings and concerns.

6 Ask them to try and reach a consensus.

7 The mixed groups take it in turns to share with the class the views they expressed and the consensus they reached.

8 Once all the groups have shared their conclusions, invite the class to reach a general consensus on the rights of both non-smokers and smokers, but acknowledging at the same time that smoking poses serious health risks.

Variation

This activity can also be used with other controversial topics, for example, students in favour of and against the death penalty, abortion, drugs, etc.

Comments

For this activity to be successful there must be at least a few smokers in the class.

1.11 The Nobel Peace Prize

This activity raises awareness of the Nobel Peace Prize. After a group fact-finding task, students prepare a profile of the ideal Nobel Peace Laureate and discuss the importance of the Nobel Peace Prize and its contribution to world peace.

Level Pre-intermediate and above

Time 40 minutes

Aims LANGUAGE Vocabulary for virtues and values.
OTHER   Raising awareness about the Nobel Peace Prize.

Materials Encyclopaedias or other relevant reference material, including the Internet if students have access.

Preparation

Write on the board the names of the following Nobel Peace Prize winners. (You may add any others who are relevant to your location or particular interests.)

Rigoberta Menchú, Mikhail Gorbachev, Amnesty International, Desmond Tutu, Lech Walesa, Nelson Mandela, Adolfo Pérez

Esquivel, The Dalai Lama, Mother Teresa of Calcutta, Joseph Rotblat, José Ramos-Horta, Betty Williams, Anwar al-Sadat, Elie Wiesel, Yasser Arafat, Menachem Begin, Martin Luther King, Willy Brandt, Eisaku Sato, Alfonso García Robles.

Procedure

1 Ask the students what they know about the Nobel Peace Prize.

2 If necessary, explain that the Nobel Peace Prize is awarded to a person or organization that has made an extraordinary contribution to world peace in the preceding year. Tell the students that all the names on the board are Nobel Peace Prize winners.

3 Arrange the class into groups and ask each group to choose one of the names on the board. Using the reference material, they should find out, and write down in note form, the following information about the Nobel Peace Prize winner they have selected:
   a Date of birth and death (if applicable)
   b Country of origin
   c Year he/she was awarded the Nobel Prize
   d His/her contribution to world peace.
   (This could be done for homework.)

4 Elicit results and write them on the board by each name.

5 Hold a whole class discussion, focusing on the following questions:
   a Why do you think the Nobel Peace Prize is important?
   b Is the country of origin of the winner (or the place where he/she lives) important? Why?
   c Do you think any of the laureates listed should not be a Nobel Peace Prize winner? Why?

6 Ask the groups to suggest the qualities of the kind of person they would like to see being awarded the next Nobel Peace Prize.

7 Draw a simple human outline on the board.

8 Choose a student to come to the board to act as a scribe.

9 Elicit results and as each group offers its opinions, ask the student at the board to write within the human outline all the good points and virtues suggested (see the example on the next page).

10 Ask the class if they can think of anybody who matches this profile.

11 Write suggestions on the board.

Follow-up 1

In groups, students can work on the design and preparation of a new School Peace Prize. They should think of criteria for the selection of candidates—the qualities required, the type of actions they should undertake or campaigns they should develop, their expected contribution to peace and understanding (for example, 'put an end to discrimination at school', 'help stop bullying', 'be supportive of his/her schoolmates').

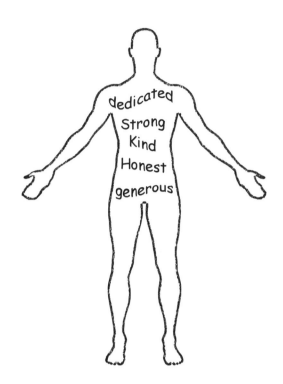

Follow-up 2

For homework, ask the students to find out individually if there have been any Nobel Peace Prize winners from their country. If so, they should prepare a brief written report including the information in step 3 (a, b, c, and d).

Follow-up 3

1   Ask each group to choose one of the Nobel Peace Prize winners they have learnt about, and to appoint a speaker, a researcher, and a scribe.

2   Ask the researcher and the scribe to work together to produce a speech of thanks for that winner for the prize-giving event. The speaker from each group delivers the speech, in the character of the winner, to the whole class.

Follow-up 4

Students suggest people they think should receive the Prize and then, with the aid of reference material, the groups assess the merits of the different candidates.

Comments

The Nobel Prize has been given each year since 1901 to six people or organizations for the highest achievement in physics, chemistry, medicine, literature, economics, and work towards world peace. Winners of the prizes are called Nobel Laureates. The prize is named after the Swedish scientist Alfred Nobel (1833–96), who invented dynamite.

1.12 Making the match

Students find out the relationship between people and concepts or world events. They use reference materials and discuss the positive or negative contribution these people have made to humanity.

Level Upper-intermediate and above

Time 40 minutes

Aims LANGUAGE Using the simple past. Defining relative clauses.
OTHER Current affairs: matching personalities with world events.

Materials Encyclopaedias, dictionaries and relevant reference materials (including the Internet if students have access); one copy of worksheet 1.12 per student.

Word store

ethnic cleansing   the Disappeared   resistance   freedom

military regime   missionary   racial equality

Nobel Peace Prize   apartheid

Preparation

1 Make one copy of Worksheet 1.12 for each student.

2 Go through all the words and concepts in the Word store, making sure all students grasp their meaning. Use simple examples as appropriate.

Procedure

1 Give a copy of Worksheet 1.12 to each student.

2 Ask them to draw a line matching each of the names in the 'People' column with one of the 'Historical events and milestones'.

3 Briefly elicit some results.

4 Put the students into pairs and ask them to compare their results.

5 Ask the pairs to choose one of the people and to find out some basic information on him/her from the reference materials. They should write two or three lines about them. (This may be done as homework.)

6 Elicit results.

7 Ask the students what they feel the contribution of these people to humankind was, either positive or negative.

8 Ask the class if they feel it is important to remember these people and events. If so, why? What could be done in their own circumstances, with local people, to achieve this?

9 Ask the students to discuss the current status of these issues. For example:

- What is the current situation with regard to apartheid?
- Is 'world peace' any nearer to being a reality?
- Are you aware of any ethnic cleansing taking place now?

Variation

You can change the names of the people and events to suit your students' curriculum or their knowledge of the world.

Follow-up 1

Ask the students to prepare an extended biography in report format on the person they selected. This should include some major events and the corresponding dates.

Follow-up 2

1 Ask each student to select one of the people and write and deliver a five-minute speech for him or her. They should choose the style of presentation (for example, a chat show, a formal interview, a conference, a demonstration, a rally, a press conference, etc.).

2 The students present their speeches in a later lesson. They can use costumes and/or make-up, and video the speeches to show to other classes.

Worksheet 1.12
Matching pieces

People	Historical events and milestones
Dalai Lama	Give Peace a Chance
Adolf Hitler	Civil Disobedience
Mahatma Gandhi	War on Afghanistan and Iraq
Augusto Pinochet	The Missionaries of Charity
Nelson Mandela	Ethnic cleansing
John Lennon	1964 Nobel Peace Prize
Mother Teresa of Calcutta	Apartheid
George W. Bush	Death under military regimes
Martin Luther King	China's invasion of Tibet

Photocopiable © Oxford University Press

Answers Dalai Lama—China's invasion of Tibet
Adolf Hitler—Ethnic cleansing
George W. Bush—War on Afghanistan and Iraq
Martin Luther King—1964 Nobel Peace Prize
Mother Teresa of Calcutta—The Missionaries of Charity
John Lennon—Give Peace a Chance
Nelson Mandela—Apartheid
Augusto Pinochet—Death under military regimes
Mahatma Gandhi—Civil Disobedience

1.13 Springboard statements

This activity presents an interesting array of statements by well known personalities which can be the starting point for individual reflection, pair and group work, and a good opportunity to raise awareness of various Global Issues.

Level Intermediate and above

Time 40 minutes +

Aims LANGUAGE Reporting statements in the students' own words.
Discussion.

OTHER Raising awareness of Global Issues.

Materials Copies of Worksheet 1.13.

Word store

communist **communism** to cherish democratic

democracy harmony **equal opportunities** consent

human rights **equality before the law** dignity

discrimination rationalization deceit revolutionary

truthful to perish constraints to redress to indemnify

way of life theft faith free compassion beggar

outrage to cope with perilous struggle tragedy

vengeful compassionate

Procedure

1 Select some of the statements in the Worksheet.

2 Put the students into pairs or groups, or if you prefer, let them work individually. Give out the Worksheets or ask the students to copy out two of the statements.

3 Read out the selected quotations to the class. Help out where necessary with difficult language or concepts.

4 Ask the class to paraphrase the statements in English, in their own words. Use the Word store for useful vocabulary.

5 Ask the students to think about the questions. Ask for feedback and write ideas on the board.

6 Encourage discussion of the issues.

Variation 1

1 Prepare slips with the quotation(s), distribute them to the students, and ask them to work in groups.

2 They reformulate the content of their statements, either orally or in writing.

Worksheet 1.13

When I give food to the poor, they call me a saint. When I ask why the poor have no food they call me a communist.
— Dom Helder Camara, Brazilian priest

1 Does the term 'communist' have a positive or a negative connotation here? Why?
2 Why is feeding the poor fine but asking why they are hungry not so acceptable?

There's enough on this planet for everyone's need but not for everyone's greed.
— Mahatma Gandhi, Indian peace activist

1 What is the difference between 'need' and 'greed'?
2 What does the statement mean? Do you agree with it?

If you think you are too small to have an impact, try going to bed with a mosquito in the room.
— Anita Roddick, founder of The Body Shop

1 What is the true meaning of this statement?
2 Can you provide a few examples in which individuals can become mosquitoes in relation to Global Issues?

Political language—and with variations this is true of all political parties—is designed to make lies sound truthful and murder respectable.
— George Orwell (1903–50), English novelist and essayist, in *Politics of the English Language*

1 How can anyone make lies sound truthful?
2 Can you think of world events which illustrate this statement?

Every gun that is made, every warship launched, every rocket fired signifies, in the final sense, a theft from those who hunger and are not fed, those who are cold and are not clothed.
— Dwight D. Eisenhower (1890–1969), former US President

1 Do you agree with this statement? Why?
2 What could be done to change this?

True compassion is more than flinging a coin at a beggar; it comes to see that an edifice which produces beggars needs restructuring.
— Rev. Dr. Martin Luther King, Jr., American civil rights campaigner

1 What is the true meaning of this statement?
2 How could the mentioned edifice be restructured?

We must be the change we wish to see.
— Mahatma Gandhi, Indian peace activist

Can you provide examples?

The outrage of hunger in a world of plenty will never be solved by 'experts' somewhere. It will only be solved when people like you or me decide to act.
— Frances Moore Lappé, contemporary US writer, nutritionist, and co-founder of Food First

How can individuals act to improve the situation described?

They were nothing more than people, by themselves. Even paired, any pairing, they would have been nothing more than people by themselves. But all together, they had become the heart and muscles and mind of something perilous and new, something strange and growing and great. Together, all together, they were instruments of change.
— Keri Hume, contemporary Maori writer, in *The Bone People*

What do you think they achieved by working together?

Variation 2

1 Reproduce the quotations in large lettering.

2 Hand out one quotation to each student, and ask them to paraphrase it in their own words and write down their explanation on a slip of paper.

3 Collect in all the slips and put up the quotations around the classroom walls.

4 Redistribute the paraphrases and ask students to find the quotation which matches their 'explanation slip'. Ask them to stand beside the quotation which matches their paraphrase and to be prepared to
a read it aloud clearly, and
b explain it and comment if they wish.

Follow-up 1

Use these statements as triggers for further work or investigation. Ask students to do some research on the author of one of the quotations. Tell them to write a brief biography including facts which they feel are relevant, and to choose a format to present this information to the class, for example, a verbal presentation, a poster presentation, or a television chat show.

Follow-up 2

Ask the students to agree on criteria to rank the statements: for example, more important, more related to present global conditions, etc. List them on the board and let the students vote.

1.14 The global quiz

A quiz based on Global Issues to help students assess their own knowledge of the world and compare their results.

Level Upper-intermediate and above

Time 40 minutes

Aims LANGUAGE Expressing opinions. Number vocabulary.

OTHER Raising awareness and assessing existing knowledge of Global Issues. Class discussion.

Materials One copy of the 'Global Issues Quiz' Worksheet per student.

> Word store
>
> processed food   genetically-modified organisms (GMOs)
> illiterate/illiteracy   debt repayment   sanctions   to impose
> terrorism   terrorist attack   AIDS   HIV   death penalty

Procedure

1 Give a copy of the Global Issues Quiz to each student. Ask them to complete it on their own.

Worksheet 1.14
Global Issues Quiz

1 What percentage of all processed foods contain genetically-modified organisms (GMOs)?

☐ 10 %   ☐ 30%   ☐ 60%

2 How many of the 6,300 million people in the world are hungry?

☐ 50 million   ☐ 100 million   ☐ 1,300 million

3 What percentage of the money the world spends on weapons a year (800 billion US dollars) would be needed to put every child into school?

☐ less than 1%   ☐ 10%   ☐ 50%

4 How many children die each year as a result of debt repayments?

☐ 500,000   ☐ 7 million   ☐ 20 million

5 How much money do developing nations spend on debt repayment for every $1 they receive in grants?

☐ $1.5   ☐ $5   ☐ $13

6 How many of the nearly 1,000 million illiterate people in the world are women?

☐ 30%   ☐ 50%   ☐ 65%

7 How many Iraqi children died as a result of the sanctions imposed by the United Nations on Iraq after the first Gulf War (1992)?

☐ 1,000   ☐ 50,000   ☐ 500,000

8 How many people were killed in the terrorist attack on the New York Twin Towers on September 11 2001?

☐ 500   ☐ 3,000   ☐ 10,000

9 How many African children under 15 suffer from AIDS?

☐ 50,000   ☐ 500,000   ☐ over 1 million

10 How many countries used the death penalty in 2002?

☐ less than 10   ☐ nearly 90   ☐ over 100

2 Check their results and share the answers with the class.

3 Hold a class debate on one or more of the questions.

Answers

1 60%,	5 $13,	8 3,000,
2 1300 million,	6 65%,	9 over 1 million,
3 less than 1%,	7 500,000,	10 nearly 90
4 7 million,		

Follow-up

Put the students into groups and ask them to choose a question. They do some research into the issue and prepare a short class presentation such as a news report, poster, oral presentation, or dramatization.

Comments

The answers were correct at the time of going to press. Please refer to the sources recommended in the Reference Library to update the information if necessary.

Recommended resources

State of the World, published every year by the Worldwatch Institute.

Global Issues website.

OneWorld website.

1.15 Global island discs

Level   Intermediate and above

Time   60 minutes over several lessons

Aims   LANGUAGE Expressing an argument.
        OTHER   Raising awareness and assessing knowledge of Global Issues.

Materials   Students will provide music and lyrics, plus brief written explanations. One photocopy of the selected lyrics per student or on transparencies to use with an overhead projector. Cassette or CD players.

Procedure

1 Explain that there is a programme on British radio which asks famous people to imagine they are stuck on a desert island. They list, play, and explain eight favourite pieces of music they would like to have with them if they were stuck alone on the island.

2 Ask the students to imagine they are stuck on a Global Island and to think of any songs they know which comment on Global Issues. They should make a few notes on why they like them. Go around helping with reasons, expressions, vocabulary and, if you feel the concept is not clear, explain that Global Issues are issues that affect large

numbers of people or the environment (for example, war, hunger, unemployment, social problems).

3 Ask the students to bring a recording of one song each to the next lesson, together with the lyrics and a brief written explanation of why each song expresses something important for them.
Note: some students may forget so it is important that you have two or three of your own available.

4 When you have collected all the songs, check that they are suitable to play in class, that the lyrics are correct, and that the students' rationales make sense.

5 In the next lesson, list all the songs (and the musicians) on the board and let the students vote for the one they would like to work with first (other than their own).

6 Return the material to the students. The presentations will take place in the order of the number of votes received. Each student introduces their song with their explanation, and hands out the lyrics or puts them on the board or OHP. They 'teach' the vocabulary and concepts, and discuss the issues.

7 If you and your students enjoy singing together, sing the song and have fun!

Follow-up 1

The students prepare a poster on their song, with lyrics, notes, and pictures of the musicians and which illustrate the issues.

Follow-up 2

Students produce a pack featuring a few songs with their lyrics, pictures, and articles or interviews, and build up a music and song archive for later use or even for other classes to use.

Follow-up 3

The students choose five or ten songs each, and design a cover and give a name to their 'compilation album'.

Follow-up 4

If the song tells a story, the class works in groups to write down and present or dramatize the story.

Recommended resources

Music and Song, RBT series, Oxford University Press.

The Rough Guide to World Music, Rough Guides Ltd.

Worlds Behind the Music, RISC.

Forty Years of Pop, Oxford University Press.

The Harmony Illustrated Encyclopedia of Rock.

1.16 Pictures and stories

Students use visual clues to find the other half of a picture which involves a Global Issue. Once found, pairs of students use prior knowledge and their imagination to create the narrative of the picture.

Level Pre-intermediate and above

Time 40 minutes

Aims LANGUAGE Describing pictures, people, and places. Discussing ideas. Taking notes.

OTHER Tapping into prior knowledge of the world; creativity.

Materials Lots of magazines featuring Global Issues in pictures/photos/advertisements.

Preparation

1 Choose a set of 'Global Issues' pictures from magazines or newspapers.

2 Cut the pictures in half horizontally or vertically, one half per student.

3 Stick the picture halves on card.

Procedure

1 Check you have an even number of students present. If not you will need to join in.

2 Shuffle the cards and hand them out.

3 Ask the students to observe their picture in silence and to make notes on the details.

4 Ask them to think about how they could describe these details to a listener.

5 Elicit ideas and make a list of tips on the board. It should include:
   • People
   • Scenery/background/context
   • Topic
   • Colour
   • Objects
   • Movement/actions
   • Writing
   • Cut-off point (i.e. the point at which the picture is cut and what the other half may look like).

6 Allow 3–5 minutes for the students to study and memorize the pictures. They then put their pictures face down on their chairs.

7 The students move around the room and talk to each other, describing their half of the picture, trying to find their partner.

8 When they have found their partner, they look at the whole picture together and discuss and write the answers to the following questions. Explain that this is not a test, but rather a means of

finding out how much they already know. They do not have to get the answers 'right' but they do have to use common sense. If they don't know the exact name of the place, for example, they should make up a suitable one.

9 Ask the pairs to share their results with the class.

Global Issues Pictures
a Where did this story take place?
b Who is involved? Name them.
c What is happening?
d Why is this happening?
e How could the situation be resolved?
f How did this picture make you feel?
g Can you find any similar situation in your life?
h Would you want to experience this? Explain.

Photocopiable © Oxford University Press

Follow-up 1

Each student writes the story of the picture as:
- a news broadcast
- a fictionalized account
- a letter to a family relative
- a letter of protest.

Follow-up 2

Ask the students to get into groups and tell each other the story of their pictures. They choose one to dramatize, finishing with the 'still' shown in the picture.

1.17 What's poverty to you?

Students define poverty then analyse the concept in more depth.

Level Pre-intermediate and above

Time 30 minutes

Aims LANGUAGE Relative clauses; modals for possibility.
OTHER Investigating the true meaning of poverty.

Materials A copy of the statement on poverty for each student.

Procedure

1 Ask the students the following questions, giving them time to think and write down a few responses:
   a Do you consider yourself to be rich or poor?
   b How much do you spend on yourself per day?
   c What do you buy?
   d Do you know anyone who is really poor?
   e What do they not have?

Word store

poverty   eradication   statistics   humiliation   powerlessness
hardship   vast   income   inequality   to halve   utopian
the means   the will   debt relief   protectionist   negligible
governance   to spare   abject   equitable

Background information

World poverty is on the increase again after 50 years of poverty
reduction. People are regarded as poor when they have no access
to the basic rights most people in the Western world take for
granted: food, shelter, clothes, proper health care, clean water,
and education.

2   Elicit answers and write them on the board.

3   Ask the students to try to define the term 'poverty' (for example,
people are poor when they have no …).

4   Elicit answers and write a few suggested definitions on the board.

5   Distribute copies of the following statement on poverty. Read the
passage together, making sure any difficult language is understood.

> Many people and organizations define 'poor' as one of the over
> 1.2 billion people (out of the world total of 6.3 billion) who live
> today on less than two dollars a day. But poverty is not about
> money. It is about access to the basic rights of food, education,
> shelter, clean water and proper health care.

6   Ask the class to discuss the following questions in pairs:
a   According to this definition, what is used to define 'poverty'?
b   Could you and your family live on less than two US dollars a day? Is
this a little or a lot of money in your country?
c   How could the world guarantee that everyone has access to the
basic rights in the statement?

7   Ask for feedback and discuss the answers briefly.

8   Put the class into small groups and ask them to brainstorm:
a   a new definition of 'poverty'
b   what could be done to fight poverty at global and local levels
c   the role governments, non-governmental organizations (NGOs),
and commercial companies should play in this.

9   Elicit results and write them up on board. Ask the students for any
ideas they would be willing to take action on.

Follow-up 1

Students find out if there are pockets of poverty in their country or in neighbouring countries. They prepare a report describing that type of poverty, either in writing as a newspaper report or orally as a newscast.

Follow-up 2

1 Students research updated statistics on world poverty and prepare a presentation.

2 Ask a few students to give their talk, paying attention to presentation skills.

Follow-up 3

1 Write on the board:

   For the first time in human history, the number of overweight people exceeds the number of underweight people.

2 Read the statement out to the class.

3 Elicit reactions and hold a class debate.

Recommended resources

NGO websites: Bread for the World; the OneWorld Net; War on Want; Global Issues.

2

Personal experiences

This chapter makes use of students' prior knowledge of the world and their personal experiences, using a variety of techniques (including trips outside the classroom) to help the students reflect on everyday events and situations related to Global Issues.

Our perception of the world and our values and attitudes are partly shaped by the information we receive and the way in which we process it, but also to a large extent by our experiences. Learning by doing is an important part of the learning process for all ages, especially for teenagers, who have a strong desire to express themselves and to assert their own emerging personalities. Students welcome every opportunity to refer to their own lives and experiences. Teachers can use this to advantage in the classroom to involve students in discussions of attitudes towards Global Issues.

2.1 Biking for clean air

In this activity, students reflect on the environmental impact of travel. They do research into the greenhouse effect and less polluting means of transport.

Level Elementary and above

Time 40 minutes

Aims LANGUAGE Using gerunds. Supporting opinions.
OTHER Raising awareness of the greenhouse effect and of our individual responsibilities in relation to this issue.

Procedure

1 Ask the students how they usually get to school or work: by bus or tram, by car or motorbike, by train/underground/metro, by bike, or on foot.

2 Ask them how they think the method of transport they use affects the environment.

3 Copy the Pollution Points table on to the board, or give it out as a worksheet. The points represent the amount of carbon dioxide generated by each method of transport over the same distance with the same number of passengers.

Energy consumption points

Walking	0 energy consumption points
Travelling by bus/tram	30 energy consumption points
Driving a car	100 energy consumption points
Travelling by plane	405 energy consumption points
Riding a bike	0 energy consumption points
Using the train/ underground	30 energy consumption points

Photocopiable © Oxford University Press

4 Explain that these energy consumption points correspond to values per vehicle over the same distance with the same number of passengers:
car (100 ÷ 4 passengers) = 25 points
bus/tram (30 ÷ 4 passengers) = 7.5 points
plane (405 ÷ 4 passengers) = 101 points

5 Ask the students to rank the methods of transport, with the one creating the least pollution at the top and the one creating the most pollution at the bottom.

6 Ask them to write their name next to the method they use most regularly.

7 Hold a general discussion on the pros and cons for both individuals and the community of using methods of transport that create less pollution. You could include how realistic it is to expect people to change their mindsets/routines/expectations: *Which of your family and friends are going to swap their car for a bike? Why? Why not?*

Follow-up 1

Students find out about the effects of exhaust fumes, relate these to global problems, and find out about less polluting alternatives to traditional methods of transport.

Follow-up 2

Ask the students to think of ideas for a campaign promoting the use of non-polluting transport (such as posters, T-shirt designs, badges, and leaflets). Invite them to put their ideas into practice by organizing a school campaign.

Recommended resources

1001 Ways to Save the Planet and *Green Living* by Bernadette Vallely.

Blueprint for a Green Planet by John Seymour and Herbert Girardet, Dorling Kindersley.

50 Simple Things You can Do to Save the Earth by the EarthWorks Group.

Causing a Stink! The Eco-warrior's Handbook for Kids, published by Friends of the Earth.

Acknowledgements

The data in the table are based on a UPI report, Heidelberg, 1989, published by the German Ministry of Transport.

2.2 Use what you've got

This is a hands-on activity in which students use items from their environment to produce a collage/drawing/composition.

Level Lower-intermediate and above

Time 120 minutes

Aims LANGUAGE Developing vocabulary and expressions to relate first-hand experiences.

OTHER To raise awareness of our need to acquire material goods and our lack of ability to be creative with what is to hand. To observe the state of the streets and to list rubbish found on the ground.

Materials 1 Pictures, postcards, examples of wall paintings, handicrafts, signs made by hand, etc.

2 Two sheets of paper per student. Pencils and glue. Green card or newspaper for mounting.

3 An area outside the school where students can work safely, such as a plaza, square, cul-de-sac, field, pedestrian walkway, or a safe street.

Preparation

Obtain permission from parents and school authorities to take the students outside the school.

Procedure

1 Explain to the students that people who do not have access to commercial art materials use whatever is to hand, using their imagination and resourcefulness to create works of art. Show examples of artwork or handicrafts made using items from the environment or recycled rubbish (see the illustration).

2 Explain that the students are going to explore artistic possibilities in their environment and at the same time make lists of all the things which should or should not be there. Ask them to prepare a sheet of paper with two columns headed 'Should' and Should Not' and take it with them to fill in on their field trip.

3 At the outdoor location, tell your students to make a drawing or collage which should fill their second sheet of paper, using only what they see around them and their own skills. They can choose any subject for their picture but no part of the sheet may be left blank.

4 They fill in their worksheet, listing items in the environment which have a right to be there (such as plants, buildings, street furniture) and items which should not be there (especially rubbish).

5　Back in the classroom, the students mount their works of art on to the green card or newspaper and make a display listing the items they used.

6　Discuss the field trip and ask the students to explain, orally or in writing, what they felt and what they have learnt from the experience. Written reports can be added to the displays.

7　Discuss the lists of 'Should' and 'Should not' and amalgamate them to form a class list. Add this to the display.

2.3　Out and about in the shopping mall

This activity encourages students to develop a critical attitude towards advertising and other promotion techniques. The activity is based on a visit to a shopping centre.

Level　Pre-intermediate and above

Time　120 minutes

Aims　LANGUAGE　Descriptions of people and places. Using *should* for recommendations.

　　　　OTHER　Analysing advertisements and branding techniques; developing critical thinking.

Materials　Copies of the worksheet.

Word store

make/brand   branding   high street shop
shopping centre/mall   target   consumer   merchandise
goods   lifestyle

Preparation

1 Visit a nearby shopping centre or mall and make sure there are plenty of shops selling clothes and other items which are likely to appeal to your students.

2 Obtain authorization from parents and school authorities, and ensure that enough assistants are available for this out-of-school activity.

Procedure

1 Explain to the students that they are going to visit a shopping centre or mall.

2 Ask them to copy the worksheet below on to a sheet of paper and duplicate it so that they have three copies in all (or provide photocopies).

3 Go through the six points on the worksheet and ensure that the students fully understand all the terms (for example, *logo, window display, accessories*).

4 Tell them that they are going to analyse some advertising techniques which often go unnoticed.

5 Make sure all the students have their worksheets. Put them in pairs and give them a deadline to finish their investigation. They should choose three shops to analyse in detail and write their findings on their worksheets. Arrange a time and place to meet before going back to school.

6 Back in class, put the students into new groups of 3 or 4 and ask them to share their findings.

7 Select a student at random to share his or her findings with the class, and list the shops surveyed on the board. Elicit from the class who else visited these and compare findings. If the class is large, focus on the three most popular shops only.

8 Ask the students to categorize the shops on the list:
   • What do they sell?
   • Are the goods they sell aimed mainly at boys or girls, or both?
   • Which were the most popular shops? Why?

9 Elicit responses to the following questions:
   a What things came up in your survey which you were not aware of before?
   b What are the element(s) (singly or combined) which actually 'sell' the product(s)?
   c Which were the most appealing shops for you, and why?

Worksheet 2.3
Out and about in the shopping mall

1 Store name Goods sold	
2 Visual imagery Photos, logos, window display, colours, etc.	
3 Persuasive elements How are customers encouraged to be part of the company's culture?	
4 Shop assistants Age, gender, outfit (formal/ informal, cost), attitude	
5 Music Type of music, lifestyle it evokes, any links between type of music and targeted consumer?	
6 Targeted consumer Describe the average consumer shopping at this store (age, income level, lifestyle, race, religion, gender)	

Follow-up 1

Ask the students to write a report using the information in their worksheets, and to add a final paragraph with recommendations or pointers for young people who may not be aware of this type of advertising (called 'immersion branding').

Follow-up 2

Ask them to reflect on this quotation, relating it to their own experience: 'One of the effects of branding is to make you feel as if you are part of a community' (Phil Knight, CEO, Nike Corporation) and to write a short piece on it.

Recommended resources

Teachable Moments section on the Media awareness website.
Ad-busters website.

We the Media published by New Press.

Acknowledgements

This activity is based on *Fish out of Water*, an activity written by media educator Carol Arcus, in the Teachable Moments section of the Media awareness website.

2.4 My personal diary

The students read passages from diaries, then relate the contents to global and other issues. The end product is an individual diary in which Global Issues are identified.

Level Intermediate and above

Time 90 minutes and subsequent short blocks of time

Aims LANGUAGE Using the simple past, simple present and present progressive, and gerunds. Expressing feelings such as fears, dreams, hopes, likes, and dislikes.

OTHER Identifying Global Issues and relating these to personal experience.

Materials Examples of diaries of each type (personal record and appointment book).

Word store

chimney pollution frizzled to get rid of instantaneously
daft swerve to miss memo expulsion aerosols
to spot check typing pool mutiny to threaten pathetic
underarm canisters limp-haired

Procedure

1 Show the students the two types of diary (personal record and appointment book) and ask what they are called in their own language and in English. Explain that in English, the term 'diary' is used to refer to both types.

2 Ask if anybody in the class writes in a diary (of any type) and ask them what sort of things they write about (for example, instructions to self, special dates to remember, homework assignments, shopping lists, things they did during the day, what made them happy/sad/angry).

3 Ask if anybody has heard of any published diaries by famous people (such as Anne Frank, a pop star, sports personality, or politician).

4 Ask why they think people write diaries and why some of them are published.

5 Explain that you (or a student) are going to read out passages from fictional examples of teenagers' diaries.

6 Distribute copies of the passages.

7 Ask for a volunteer to do the reading, or read the diaries yourself (or play an audio version—see Recommended Resources).

8 Check that all the vocabulary is understood and also make sure they grasp what worries the three teenagers mentioned in the first passage (Peter, Sally, and Sam) and Brown in the second and third.

9 List the concerns on the board.

10 Ask the students whether they have similar worries or if they know of others who do.

11 Ask the students to choose partners they can trust, and to discuss their own worries, fears, and dreams. If this makes them feel too uncomfortable, they can write them down instead.

Variation

Instead of having students write individual diaries, you could start a class diary in which global concerns are regularly included (including current affairs and information from other sources).

Follow-up 1

1 Ask them to start writing a daily or weekly diary (a personal record), including what makes them feel worried, angry, happy, sad, optimistic, etc. Invite them to reflect on whether these things or events only affect them or if they can be considered Global Issues (i.e. whether they have the potential to affect large numbers of people or the environment).

2 Make it clear that they can decide whether to share part or all of their writing with the rest of the class or with you, the teacher, or to keep it private. Also make it clear that diaries will *not* be corrected for spelling or grammar.

Follow-up 2

Divide the class into groups of three and have them improvise the conversation between Peter, Sam, and Sam's dad, or Mr Brown and two of the office workers.

Follow-up 3

Ask the students to read published diaries (see the suggestions below) and discuss them at a later date.

Recommended resources

Appel, J. 1995. *Diary of a Language Teacher*. Heinemann.

Coppard, Y. 1995. *Great! You've Just Ruined the Rest of my Life*. Puffin.

Filipovic, Z. 1995. *Zlata's Diary: A Child's Life in Sarajevo*. Penguin.

Frank, A. 1995. *The Diary of a Young Girl*. Doubleday.

Macfarlane, A. and McPherson, A. 1987. *The Diary of a Teenage Health Freak.* Oxford University Press.

Rocklin, R. 1993. *For Your Eyes Only.* Scholastic.

Townsend, S. 1989. *True Confessions of Adrian Mole.* Methuen; 1982. *The Secret Diary of Adrian Mole Aged 13¾.* Arrow; 1984. *The Growing Pains of Adrian Mole.* Methuen.

Some of these are available in audio versions.

Passage 1

Monday 9th September

Passed through Birmingham on the way—really depressing, endless rows of dirty chimneys polluting the atmosphere. Sam's dad said pollution wasn't the only thing that affected people's health around here. Unemployment was a major health problem as well.

Sam's more worried about the BOMB. He said if we were lucky we wouldn't know anything about it, we'd just get frizzled up instantaneously. Randy Jo said he thought it would be a good idea if there WAS a war as it would get rid of unemployment, either by killing us all or by us all having to fight in the army. He thinks the last world war looks really great from the television series. This daft idea made Sam's dad swerve across the road nearly crashing into the back of a huge transporter lorry carrying Japanese cars. He just missed.

From *The Diary of a Teenage Health Freak* by Aidan Macfarlane and Ann McPherson (Oxford University Press, 1987: page 91).

Passage 2

Wed July 12th

Brown has sent a memo round to all departments ordering the expulsion of all aerosols in the building. A spot check will be carried out tomorrow. The typing pool are in an ugly mood and are threatening mutiny.

Passage 3

Thursday July 13th

There were pathetic scenes throughout the day as workers tried to hang on to their underarm deodorants and canisters of hairspray. But by four o'clock Brown announced a victory. It was a perspiring and limp-haired crowd of workers who left the building. Some shook their fists at the sky and swore at the ozone layer, or the lack of it. One or the other.

From *True Confessions of Adrian Albert Mole* by Sue Townsend (Methuen/Mandarin, 1989: page 92).

2.5 Made of what?

In this activity students do research into the raw materials used in items they enjoy (such as CDs, cassettes, or minidisks) and where they come from.

Level Lower-intermediate and above

Time 40 minutes

Aims LANGUAGE Use of *comes from, is made of*; passive voice.
OTHER Reflecting on the use of raw materials; introducing or reviewing the concepts of recycling and re-using.

Materials Packaging from blank or pre-recorded cassettes or minidisks; one CD, cassette or minidisk for each student; the worksheet below; encyclopaedias and dictionaries; access to the Internet if available.

Word store

to recycle   recyclable   to re-use   re-usable

natural resources   manufacturing   to source   source

raw materials   packaging

Preparation

1 Ask the students to bring to class a blank or pre-recorded cassette, DVD, CD, or minidisk.

2 Make a copy of the worksheet for each student.

Procedure

1 Put the students into groups of three and ask them to list all the materials used to make their disk or cassette: case, wrapping, inlay, insert or label, the disk or cassette itself with all its components such as tape and screws. (See below for a guide.)

2 Draw a table on the board like the one on p. 6o and fill in some of the columns with answers from the students.

3 Once several materials have been listed, give out copies of the table and ask the students to work on their own and to think about where these come from: for example, *The CD book is made of paper, paper is made of wood, wood comes from trees.* Ask them to use the reference materials and to write their findings on the table. (They could do this step for homework.) Students may have more difficulties when dealing with steel, plastic, and other materials.

4 When most of the information has been found, bring the class together to complete all the columns on the board and comment on their findings.

Worksheet 2.5

Item	Components	Raw materials (is made of ...)	Sources
CD	Case Book Insert CD		
Cassette	Box Label Cassette itself Tape Screws		

Follow-up

Students can do some research on how much of the materials used in items they regularly consume/use is recyclable or re-usable. To find this information they could contact local or international NGOs (non-governmental organizations) or local government bodies that deal with waste. They could produce a brief written report with their findings.

Recommended resources

50 Simple Things Kids can Do to Save the Earth, by the EarthWorks Group.

Blueprint for a Green Planet, by John Seymour and Herbert Girardet.

The Young Oxford Book of Ecology, by Michael Scott.

2.6 Crossing out violent toys

Students investigate how items purchased as toys or games may promote violence.

Level Lower-intermediate and above

Time 40 minutes

Aims LANGUAGE *To make someone do something.* Toy vocabulary and brand names.

OTHER Reflecting on violence and violent toys.

Procedure

1 Draw a grid on the board with at least twice as many squares as there are students in your class (i.e. 64 squares for 32 students).

2 Elicit from students their ideas about the meaning of violence and different types of violence (physical and emotional).

3 Ask the class whether they think there is a link between children playing war games or with violent toys and violence.

4 Hold a brief discussion.

5 Ask a few students to come, one by one, to the board and to write in an empty grid square each the name of a toy or a video game based on 'killing' or 'wounding'. Names cannot be repeated.

6 Read out all the names and elicit their aims and ask the students what these games/toys do or involve (for example, cutting heads off, kicking, shooting).

7 Now ask students to come to the board and write the names of toys and games that promote peaceful play and co-operation. As they write, the students should explain their choice and cross out the name of one of the violent toys or games.

8 Ask if they have any anecdotes they would like to share. Encourage a general discussion on the advertising of these kinds of toys and games, and on their views regarding this issue.

Variation

This activity can also be done using other criteria, as, for example, toys and games based on stereotypes or sexist assumptions (for example, boys should be macho and girls docile; different packaging colours for boys' and girls' toys and games).

Follow-up

Ask the students to visit a toy shop for homework and to do a survey: do war toys and games represent a majority or a minority of the total? Are there any toys or games that specifically promote peace or co-operation?

Recommended resources

Websites: Peace Pledge Union, Media Channel, Adbusters, and Consumers International.

2.7 Supermarket detectives

Students visit a supermarket and analyse advertising incentives on product labels, such as free gifts and competitions.

Level	Lower-intermediate and above
Time	40 minutes in class
Aims	LANGUAGE Vocabulary found on product labels.
	OTHER To raise consumer awareness and promote awareness of hidden messages on labels.
Materials	Worksheet (see page 63).

Word store

giveaway   freebie   incentive   prize   competition   quality
to compromise   trade-off   dairy   soft drink   aisle   sector

Procedure
Lesson 1

1 Tell the students they are going to visit a supermarket. Ask them to team up with someone who lives near them.

2 Give out copies of the 'Supermarket detectives' worksheet, or ask the students to copy it from the board. They will need one each as they will write their findings individually.

3 Ask them to visit their local supermarket out of school hours. They should identify products with the features on the worksheet, and fill in all the boxes. Tell them the best areas of the supermarket to look at are those where dairy products, biscuits/cookies, snacks and sweets, cereals, soft drinks, and juices are displayed. Allow a few days so everyone has the chance to do the activity properly.

Lesson 2

1 The students bring back their completed worksheets and share their information with the rest of the class.

2 Elicit comments and conclusions. The questions below may be of help:
   a What age of customers are these products aimed at?
   b Why do manufacturers use these types of incentives?
   c On what basis do you decide which product to buy? Quality? Price? Presentation? Free gifts?

Follow-up 1

Ask the students to design labels for products featuring other messages they think are worth promoting. They can use drawings, pictures, and slogans.

Follow-up 2

If the labels are in your students' mother tongue, ask them to redesign them in English, using a dictionary if necessary.

Recommended resources

Websites: Consumers International, Global Issues.

Worksheet 2.7:
Supermarket detectives

	Product 1	Product 2
Features cartoon or film characters or celebrities		
Offers free gifts		
Invites you to take part in competitions		
Tokens to collect		
Other promotions, e.g discounts, two-for-the-price-of-one, etc.		

Photocopiable © Oxford University Press

2.8 The colour of your coffee

Students reflect on world trade injustices using a primary commodity, coffee, to trigger discussion about the role played by consumers in maintaining or changing the status quo. The concept of *fair trade* is introduced in the follow-up.

Level	Intermediate and above
Time	40 minutes

Aims   LANGUAGE   Names of countries; modals, especially *could* to express possibility.

         OTHER   To raise awareness of world trade imbalances and social injustices.

Materials   One small world map per group or a large one (preferably Peters Projection), reference materials (for example, literature produced by NGOs such as CAFOD), encyclopaedias, one empty coffee jar or bag per student, copies of the Coffee Worksheet and Coffee Information Box.

Background information

Trade has been a fundamental development tool for peoples all over the globe since ancient times. However, not all trade benefits all parties involved, and not all trade is fair. Some corporations take advantage of their political or financial strength to impose on others trade conditions that only worsen the situation of the weakest. The Fair Trade movement is an international campaign/trade policy which aims to pay producers a fair price for their products, considering other factors in setting prices than the 'market price' (usually set by powerful companies).

Word store

product   commodity   producer   trade   consumer   harvest

geographical   political   developmental   features   growers

export(ers)   ship(pers)   roast(ers)   retailers   **fair trade**

staple/cash crops   loans   **global market**   labour   **free trade**

brand

Preparation

1 Ask each student to bring to class an empty coffee jar or bag. You should bring some too in case some students forget.

2 Put up the world map and the Coffee Information Box on the board or wall.

3 Make photocopies of simple world maps and the Coffee Worksheet, or copy this on to the board.

Procedure

1 Give out copies of the Coffee Information Box or ask the students to look at the display.

2 Ask the students to copy the Coffee Worksheet from the board, or hand out photocopies.

3 Put the students in groups according to the number of jars or bags available. Ask them to find out where the coffee was grown, and to find those countries on the world map.

4 Ask them to complete the worksheets. Go round monitoring and helping with any problems.

5 Elicit feedback and comments from the class. The following questions can be used as a guide:
   • What are the shared features of the growing countries?
   • How far are they from your country?
   • Are you from/in any of the grower countries?

Coffee information box

- Biggest producers: Brazil (1.3 million tonnes), Colombia (780,000 tonnes), and Indonesia (390,000 tonnes).
- Annual world production: 5.6 million tonnes.
- There are 41 producer countries in the world.
- Main consumer countries: USA (22% of total), Germany (16%), France (7.6%).
- Coffee is the most important internationally traded commodity after oil.
- Coffee is the second largest source of Third World export earnings.
- Coffee only grows in the tropics.
- Profit shares information: growers 10%, exporters 10%, shippers and roasters 55%, retailers 25%.

Photocopiable © Oxford University Press

(**Note**: if you happen to be in a grower country or if you have students from grower countries, you could ask them to provide first-hand information on whether people there drink a lot of coffee, how it is made, etc.)

The students do research into the coffee industry and produce a poster or leaflet.

Variation

Ask groups of students to research the trade situation for other products, such as chocolate, clothes, trainers, bananas, or spices.

Follow-up

Expand the scope of this activity by researching the Fair Trade movement (what it is, why it was developed) and the products available in your country (if any), where they are exported to and from, etc.

Recommended resources

The A to Z of World Development (New Internationalist).

The *Global Issues for Learners of English* section of the New Internationalist website.

One World website.

Labour Behind the Label.

XChanging the World resource pack produced by RISC/VSO.

Trading Training Game by CAFOD and Christian Aid.

NGOS: Fair Trade Foundation UK, The Max Havelaar Foundation, Make Trade Fair.

Worksheet 2.8
Coffee

1 Brand name _____

   Country where coffee is grown _____

   Country where coffee is processed/packaged _____

   Country where coffee is sold _____

2 Features shared by coffee growing countries:

   Geographical _____

   Physical _____

   Developmental _____

   Other _____

3 a What do you think about the fact that only 10 per cent of what you pay for
      your instant coffee goes to the people that spend their lives growing and
      harvesting it?

      _____

      _____

   b How might natural disasters affect the lives of growers?

      _____

      _____

   c What could you do as a consumer to improve this situation?

      _____

      _____

   d Why do you think most coffee consumer countries import raw coffee beans and
      carry out other processes, such as roasting, at home?

      _____

      _____

2.9 Many cultures, one world

Students think about the music they like, the role of music, and its potential to promote cross-cultural understanding. By identifying bands and musicians who sing about social issues, students are exposed to not only world music and relevant Global Issues, but also to language.

Level Upper-intermediate and above

Time At least 40 minutes in class plus survey time

Aims LANGUAGE Expressing likes and dislikes. Reading for clues. Reading CD and record covers and contents for gist.

OTHER Raising cultural awareness, establishing links between local bands and others from other countries/cultures.

Materials Survey table to tabulate information; information on WOMAD (World of Music, Arts and Dance—a festival which takes place every year in Reading, UK, and also in other parts of the world and whose aim is to promote, maintain, improve, and advance education on world cultures).

Preparation

Download information from the Internet on WOMAD, or visit the World Music section of a local music store.

Procedure

1 Write the following questions on the board. Ask the students to take two minutes' silent time, thinking on their own and making notes on the questions.
   - What kind of music do you like?
   - When do you listen to it?
   - Where are your favourite bands or musicians from?
   - What do you think is the purpose of music?

2 Appoint a scribe to write on the board and elicit from the class different kinds of music they know (for example, rap, rock, pop, garage, classical, traditional, folk, acid house, reggae, grunge, ska).

3 Ask the class what they think the aims of music are (for example, entertainment, expression of something, rituals and ceremonies). To encourage discussion you can introduce the important role played by music in different cultures.

4 Put the students into pairs. Ask them to draw two columns on a piece of paper and write a list of band names and titles of songs which protest against things like war, social injustice, discrimination, racism, or violence.

5 Ask them to think of all the issues that bands could choose to write and record songs about (for example, love, hunger, war, bullying).

6 Elicit feedback from the class.

7 Divide the class into two halves, A and B.

8 For homework, ask the students in group A to survey local music shops for the names of musicians who sing in English about social problems. They should include bands and artists who are clearly part of western culture. Group B will focus on musicians whose records are usually displayed in the *World Music* or *Ethnic* section who sing about Global Issues, not necessarily in English.

9 Ask the students to complete the World Music worksheet.

10 In the next lesson, the students report on their findings. Hold a discussion about the role played by musicians in raising awareness of social issues. The questions below can be used as a guide:
- What countries/cultures are represented?
- Do they sing about the same things?
- In addition to the CD labels, what other sources could you use to find out more about these bands and musicians?

Worksheet 2.9
World music

Band	CD/tape / record	Country/ culture	Social issues addressed	Can you tell from album or song names? If so, which one/s?
Yothu Yindi	Freedom	Australian aborigine	freedom	Album title: *Freedom*

Photocopiable © Oxford University Press

Follow-up 1

1 Invite the students to vote for the band/song they would most like to listen to and work on in class, and ask them to provide you with the CD or cassette and lyrics.

2 If the lyrics are suitable for use in a school, make a copy for each student, and decide on how you are going to work on the song. (For song exploitation techniques please refer to Chapter 4).

Follow-up 2

Expand the scope of this activity by asking the students to do a mini-survey on any band or musician from the **majority world** and to write a simple report on their main characteristics (name,

country/culture of origin, social standing, album names, type of
music played).

Recommended resources
Websites: Reading International Solidarity Centre (RISC), WOMAD.
The Rough Guide to World Music published by Rough Guides Ltd.

2.10 Deconstructing bullying

**Using a simple building block game, students reflect on bullying,
and on possible ways of fighting this problem.**

Level   Lower-intermediate and above

Time   40 minutes

Aims   LANGUAGE Modals and gerunds.
   OTHER   Raising awareness on bullying and on what can be done
   to fight it.

Materials   A number of building blocks (Lego™ type), preferably coloured.
Prepare a large base so that it does not collapse after a few blocks
have been put in place.

Word store
deconstruct   bully   **bullying**   to push around   hit   coward
goody-goody   gang   inferior   superior   power

Procedure

1   Explain the meaning of 'bullying' and 'to bully'.

2   Ask for the students' opinions on the topic, and whether any
students are willing to tell anecdotes about bullies and bullying
(stress that no names may be mentioned). Ask if they have ever read
any stories, poems, or plays about the topic.

3   Put the students into groups of three and ask them to brainstorm on
what kinds of actions, words, or attitudes constitute 'bullying'. Each
group makes notes.

4   Place all the building blocks on your desk.

5   The groups take it in turns to send one student to the front.

6   They share with the class one of the elements of 'bullying' that they
identified in their group, and put one block on the pile to make a
tower.

7   When everybody has contributed to the 'bullying tower', ask the
groups to brainstorm on what can be done to eliminate bullying.

8   Write on the board all the modals students have learnt: for example,
could, should, would, must, can, might.

9   The groups think of sentences using one of the modals to write a
short sentence showing what can be done to fight bullying.

Example Bullies should have to listen to victims to understand the effects of what they have done.

10 Each group sends a representative to write one of their sentences on the board. They then take one block off the pile for each idea on how to counter bullying. Hopefully the whole tower will be 'deconstructed' by the end.

11 Elicit class reactions.

12 Produce a class poster with recommendations for reducing bullying.

Follow-up

Students do some research into organizations which work to educate bullies and to stop bullying in their own area/country.

Comment

This is an effective, graphic way of showing how a seemingly intractable problem can literally be made smaller.

Recommended resources

Websites: Success Unlimited; Childline, Kidscape.

2.11 Let's imagine how you live

Students think about how people from other cultures live. By referring to their own daily activities first, and then visualizing people in other cultures, students are encouraged to understand more about diversity.

Level Lower-intermediate and above

Time 60 minutes

Aims LANGUAGE Describing everyday activities.
OTHER To raise awareness of cultures other than students' own.

Materials Information cards on different cultures with facts on the way they live.

Word store

to visualize   routine   senses   peoples   cultures

indigenous   Aborigines   Indians   housing   **environment**

Preparation

1 Prepare information cards with basic factual information and pictures on a number of cultures/peoples different from your own. The information should give an idea of how these people live, what their homes and immediate environment are like, and so on.

2 Make enlargements of the cards for class display.

Procedure

1 Write on the board the following headings:

Things I eat
Things I see
Things I hear
My home is …

2 Ask the students to take several blank sheets of paper and to draw a vertical line down the centre of each sheet, dividing them into two. Tell them to label the top of the left-hand column with their own name.

3 Tell them to copy the headings on to the left-hand side of their sheets, leaving space for writing between the headings.

4 Ask the students to close their eyes and to think for a moment about their daily routine from the time they wake up until the evening. Tell them to visualize what they do and to think of the things they see, eat, and hear, and about their home. They open their eyes.

5 Now ask them to write the things they visualized under the headings on the left-hand side of their sheets.

Example Things I eat
Toast with marmalade for breakfast
Curry and rice for lunch

My home is
A large detached house with four bedrooms, two bathrooms, a kitchen/a tall block of flats/a small stone cottage.

6 Ask them to think of a person of their own age from any of the cultures/peoples on which there is an information card. They read the card and go through their daily routines again, this time trying to visualize what the other person might do, eat, and hear, what his/her home is like, and so on.

7 Ask them to write the information in the right-hand column of their sheets.

8 Ask the students to swap their sheets with a neighbour and to try to identify the culture/people. They discuss their guesses and why they put what they did.

Variation

Instead of preparing information cards yourself you can ask the students to prepare them in advance, giving them a wide choice of cultures/peoples. They can use this information for themselves or they can swap cards.

2.12 Agony Aunt Angie

Students read and analyse passages from advice columns in newspapers or magazines and write their own, focusing on Global Issues.

Level Intermediate and above

Time 40 minutes

Aims LANGUAGE Asking questions, asking for advice. Use of modals for advice.

OTHER Thinking about personal and global concerns.

Materials Examples of agony columns from magazines and newspapers.

Background information

Many popular magazines have a special column where readers write to an expert for advice on problems (usually personal, emotional, sexual, or health questions). The letters are usually quite short and the expert answers 'in person'.

Preparation

Collect 'agony' or advice columns from magazines or newspapers. Make enough copies for your students.

Procedure

1 Give each student an agony column letter and reply. Read a few out loud and discuss the nature of the problems and the suggested solutions. Encourage the students to see the problems as personal and the answers as general.

2 Ask the students to think about the extent to which it is possible to find a simple solution to another person's problems.

3 Ask them how they try to solve their personal problems, and if they go to experts or family or friends.

4 Put the students in pairs and ask them to:
   a write to 'Agony Aunt Angie' about a global issue rather than a personal problem
   b swap their letter with another pair, and to write answers
   c find a suitable name for the column on global problems
   d present the question and answer to the class.

Follow-up 1

The students do a role play using problems and solutions as the basis for a television interview with an 'expert' on the issue.

Follow-up 2

This activity can become part of 2.13, 'Global Issues class magazine'.

2.13 Global Issues class magazine

The end product of this co-operative activity is a class magazine on Global Issues with students deciding the contents. Products from other activities in this book can contribute to the magazine.

Level Elementary to advanced

Time At least 3 hours plus homework time; or as an ongoing project over a term or course

Aims LANGUAGE Writing genres: informative, argumentative, letters to the editor, reporting, advertisements, agony columns.

OTHER Analysing the content and layout of magazines.

Materials Lots of magazines, pictures, paper, pens, computers (if available), staplers.

Preparation

Ask students to bring in a selection of magazines. Bring some yourself, including if possible some on Global Issues such as *New Internationalist*.

Procedure

1 Tell the class that they are going to produce a class magazine as an ongoing project. Ask them to form groups which are convenient for them to work together in, out of school as well as in class.

2 Analyse the magazines under the following headings:
  a Front and back cover: for example, logo, title, artwork, colours used, date, price, bar code, headlines, ISSN.
  b Editorial
  c Contents page
  d Type, number, style, and layout of articles (for example, feature articles, short items, news, interviews, reviews)
  e Type, number, style, and layout of advertisements
  f Proportion of visual images to print
  g Special offers, free gifts, competitions
  h Classified advertisements and announcements (if relevant).

3 Tell the students that they are going to produce a class magazine on Global Issues. They can decide what topics to cover: for example, whether to focus on one issue or whether to cover Global Issues in general. Ask the groups to brainstorm and make notes on the contents they would like their GI magazine to have, for example: editorial; features on major GI-related problems such as serious problems concerning the school, community, or world; news on campaigns; book, film, and music reviews; agony column (see 2.12); a Global Issues quiz; competitions of different kinds—crosswords, writing, drawing, etc.

4 The class should agree on the overall contents. Allocate one section or topic to each group (you may need to adjust the number of groups or the contents).

5　The students can include reports or fact files produced in other activities in this book (for example, 3.4, 'Questioning GMOs', 2.6, 'Crossing out violent toys', 1.1, 'Your footprint on the Earth', 1.15, 'Global Island Discs', 1.11, 'The Nobel Peace Prize', 2.12, 'Agony Aunt Angie', or 3.6, 'Our Campaign against war'.

6　Agree on deadlines for individual items and sections. You will need to check on progress regularly, and set aside time for feedback and queries.

7　The groups plan their sections, and start collecting information and pictures.

8　They report back to the class on what they plan to include in their sections. The class contributes ideas and suggests changes.

9　Each article should be read by another group for a fresh eye. If computers are available, each group writes their article in electronic form and brings it to class for editing and proof-reading. If not, produce neat final versions by hand or on a typewriter.

10　The students contribute design and illustration ideas, and produce a rough page plan or sketch of the layout.

11　If you have desktop publishing software, you can use it to collate all the articles on to one document and lay them out. Alternatively, gather all the items together and organize a layout and paste-up session.

12　Proof-read the magazine yourself.

13　Have it photocopied.

14　Distribute it to other students and parents, or sell it to create funds for charity, the school, or a club.

3

Major Global Issues

In this book we define Global Issues as 'issues that affect (or have the potential to affect) large numbers of people, animals, or the environment worldwide'. This definition is intended to help teachers and students grasp their relevance and scope. We have selected issues for this chapter that represent, in our view, concerns which have gained global relevance in recent times.

As world events and circumstances change over time, some issues will grow or reduce in importance, but in general terms we feel that those we have selected for this chapter are likely to remain of interest or even gain more relevance. However, in most cases the techniques are adaptable to other topics of interest or relevance.

Activities included in this chapter address issues such as child labour (3.13, 'Child labour in focus'), war/peace (3.6, 'Our campaign against war', and 3.7, 'The classroom for peace'), human rights (3.1, 'Identify your rights'), racism—working on a speech by Martin Luther King (3.8, 'Say no to racism'), homelessness—analysing the physical, emotional, and social needs met by a home (3.10, 'What is a home?'), and genetically-modified organisms (3.4, 'Questioning GMOs'), among others.

3.1 Identify your rights

This activity introduces the concept of human rights and encourages students to reflect on their individual rights and to establish a link between these and events in the news.

Background information

After the UN Declaration of Human Rights was drawn up in 1948, human rights violations decreased significantly in various parts of the world. However, in the world there still are over 800 million illiterate adults, nearly 160 million malnourished children under the age of five, over 20 million refugees, and 1.3 billion people living below the poverty line.

Level   Intermediate and above

Time   40 minutes

Aims LANGUAGE Reading for gist. Making an oral summary.

OTHER Identifying human rights abuses. Media literacy.

Materials News cuttings, headlines, or short news articles addressing human rights issues (in English preferably but not necessarily). There should be at least twice the number of cuttings as groups of students. Pieces of card or paper for mounting. Blank cards and one felt tip pen per group. Tape or 'Blu-Tack' for sticking posters to the walls.

Preparation

1 Collect news cuttings over a period of time (see Introduction). Mount them on separate sheets of paper or card, and hang them on the wall.

2 If you can, get hold of a copy of the UNHCR DVD/Video on human rights (see the Reference Library).

Procedure

1 Ask the students to take two minutes' silent time, thinking on their own, and to make notes on the question:

What are the things you believe you have a right to do?

2 Ask the students if they know what human rights are, and to suggest some examples. Write these on the board or on a wall poster.

3 Draw the students' attention to the newspaper cuttings on the wall and give them a few minutes to skim and scan them. They can ask questions if they need any vocabulary or concepts clarified.

4 Arrange the class into small groups. Give out a few blank cards and a felt tip pen to each group.

5 One member of each group selects a news item to take back to the group.

6 Ask the students to read their news cutting and to identify any human rights abuses in it. If they find one they write it on a blank card and pin it up next to the article.

7 Point to each human rights violation and ask the groups to summarize their news item and explain the human right they found.

Follow-up 1

Show the UNHCR video to link the abstract notion of human rights with real life.

Follow-up 2

Ask the students to prepare individual reports on the history of the Universal Declaration of Human Rights: Which are the signatory countries? Has their own country signed it? When was it drawn up? What is the aim of the Declaration?

Recommended resources

Video available free of charge from your local United Nations representative: contact them via the United Nations High Commission on Refugees (UNHCR) website (see the Reference Library, page 143).

The United Nations Universal Declaration of Human Rights (see the UN website).

Equal Rights, published by Franklin Watts.

Learning to Participate, published by Birmingham DEC.

Developing Rights, published by OXFAM.

Amnesty International website.

Human Rights Watch website.

3.2 Globalization

Students think of events or situations that might be associated with 'globalization', and play a language game. As a follow-up, they compare the GDPs of selected countries with the sales figures of some transnational corporations.

Level Intermediate and above

Time 30 minutes

Aims LANGUAGE   Speaking, writing.
OTHER   Thinking about the issue of globalization; analysing a statistical table; discussing pros and cons.

Materials One copy of the table per student.

Procedure

1 Ask the students if they know what 'globalization' means. Write some of their ideas on the board.

2 Divide them into groups of up to four.

3 Ask them to think of things, events, or situations that could be associated with globalization and to write these down.

Examples
- the Internet
- satellite television
- the relatively free flow of money and goods from country to country
- the availability of products from distant parts of the world
- the increased presence of foreign companies in any given country.

4 Now ask them to think about the advantages and disadvantages of each. Write a few examples on the board for reference.

Example *The Internet*
Pro: it helps us to find information about almost anything in the whole world.
Con: small children can get into pornographic websites.

5 Play 'Fortunately … Unfortunately'. Give the students 'think time' of about five minutes to write statements which they will read out to the class, using upwards intonation for the first sentence and downwards intonation for the second.

Example   Fortunately, large drug companies now have the resources to develop drugs to treat diseases like AIDS. **Unfortunately**, they charge so much money for the drugs that the people who need them most can't afford them.

6   The class votes for the most interesting or ironic statement.

Follow-up

1   Give each student a copy of the table and explain what GDP stands for (*Gross Domestic Product*, the total value of goods and services produced by a country in one year).

2   Ask them to analyse the table and to discuss its implications.

Recommended resources

UN *Human Development Report*, published annually by Oxford University Press.

The World Bank's *World Development Report*, published annually by Oxford University Press.

A–Z *of World Development*, published by the New Internationalist.

Globalization by Manfred B. Steger, Oxford University Press, 2003, ISBN 019 280359X.

The Breakdown of Nations by Leopold Khor, published by Green Books, ISBN 1 870 098 98 6.

The No-Nonsense Guide to Globalisation, published by New Internationalist.

The Global Issues website.

Song: NPWA (*No Power Without Accountability*) by Billy Bragg.

Table   A comparison of the GDP of selected countries and the sales of transnational corporations

	Country	GDP (in millions of dollars)	Corporation	Sales (in millions of dollars)
1	Denmark	174,363	General Motors	176,558
2	Poland	154,146	Wal-Mart	166,809
3	Malaysia	74,634	Siemens	75,337
4	Chile	71,092	Hitachi	71,858
5	Hungary	48,355	Credit Suisse	49,362

Source: Sales: *Fortune*, July 31 2000; GDP: World Bank *World Development Report* 2000, cited in *Globalization* by Manfred B. Steger, Oxford University Press, 2003, p. 49.

3.3 AIDS today

In this activity students test their knowledge and do research on AIDS.

Level   Intermediate and above

Time   40 minutes in class plus research time off-school hours

Aims   LANGUAGE   Working with acronyms, writing, speaking.

OTHER   Reflecting on the implications of AIDS and on the unequal opportunities people have in relation to this issue.

Materials   Copies of the AIDS Quiz on the next page.

Background information:

84 per cent of the world's deaths from AIDS have been in Africa and 90 per cent of babies with AIDS are born in Africa. So far, more than 14 million people have died of AIDS in Africa. AIDS drugs are manufactured by multinational pharmaceutical corporations who are unwilling to give African governments full control of these drugs.

Procedure

Lesson 1

1   Check that the students know the acronym AIDS in English. You can use the following definition:

AIDS = **A**cquired **I**mmune **D**eficiency **S**yndrome. An illness that attacks the body's ability to resist infection and which usually causes death

---

Source: *Oxford Advanced Learner's Dictionary*

2   Give out copies of the AIDS Quiz and ask the students to answer it in pairs.

3   Get them to check their answers. How many did they get right?

Answer key   1 a; 2 c; 3 c; 4 a; 5 c.

4   For homework, ask the students to do some research into AIDS. Divide the class into groups of three and give each group one question to research.

5   Agree a date when they will bring in their findings and discuss the issue.

AIDS Quiz

1 The virus that spreads AIDS is called:
   a HIV
   b TRIP
   c INSULIN

2 More than 80 per cent of the world's deaths from AIDS have been in:
   a Europe
   b North America
   c Africa

3 AIDS drugs are:
   a very cheap
   b free
   c very expensive

4 AIDS drugs are manufactured by:
   a multinational pharmaceutical companies
   b local governments
   c the World Health Organization (WHO)

5 AIDS can be transmitted:
   a by touching an AIDS-infected person
   b through food and drinks
   c through sex and needles

Questions

a How is AIDS transmitted?
b What areas of the world are the most affected by AIDS?
c What can you do at a personal level to avoid AIDS?
d How can the spread of AIDS be stopped?
e What are the main problems people face if they suffer from AIDS?

Lesson 2

6 Ask each group to present their findings.

7 Hold a class brainstorm to think of answers to the questions:
   • What (else) could be done to help African people stop the AIDS epidemic?
   • Does the international community have any responsibility?

Follow-up

In groups, the students think about how they could dramatize a situation regarding AIDS, using information from the quiz and the questions they have researched (doing role play, using puppets, etc.). They can do this for themselves or decide if they want to show it to an audience.

(See Chapter 4: Music, drama, and communication skills in Global Issues for ideas.)

Recommended resources

Websites (see the Reference Library for addresses):

The New Internationalist: go to *Global Issues for Learners of English* > *Issues* > *Africa* > *AIDS in Africa*.

AIDS Action.

AIDS.ORG.

Film: *Philadelphia*.

Songs: *Philadelphia* by Bruce Springsteen
          The Needle and the Damage Done by Neil Young.

3.4 Questioning GMOs

The students read articles for or against **genetically-modified organisms** (GMOs) and find out more information on the issue, then hold a class debate.

Level Intermediate and above

Time 15 minutes for the worksheet
20 minutes for reading and discussion
40 minutes for the debate

Aims LANGUAGE Using persuasive language: arguments for and against a topic.

OTHER Finding information about genetically-modified organisms (GMOs) and discussing their potential risks and/or benefits.

Materials One copy of worksheet 3.4 for each student; a news article for each group (see Preparation).

Background information

Pro-GMO arguments: increased crop yields, less dependence on pesticides, GMOs could help to solve the problem of world hunger

Anti-GMO arguments: loss of biodiversity, not yet fully tested for health and environmental risks, genetic contamination, transnational corporations in control of world food resources

---

Preparation

1 Find several short articles with information on GMOs (especially some on their alleged benefits and disadvantages). The Internet is a good source of information.

2 Make a copy of the worksheet for each student.

Procedure

1 Put the students into groups of four. Give each student a copy of the worksheet.

2 In their groups, the students complete the worksheet. Check their answers.

3 Ask the students if they have any views regarding genetically-modified organisms (GMOs), if they have read anything about their potential benefits or risks, etc. If some students are knowledgeable about the issue, ask them to share information with the rest of the class.

4 Divide the class into halves (A and B), and then divide each big group into smaller ones.

5 Give each A subgroup a pro-GMO article and each B subgroup an anti-GMO article.

6 Ask the groups to discuss their articles. Elicit reactions.

7 For homework, students in the A sub-groups do some more in-depth research into GMOs from the perspective of non-governmental organizations (NGOs) such as Greenpeace or Friends of the Earth. The B groups do the same but from the perspective of biotechnology companies which produce GMOs, such as Monsanto, Bayer Cropscience, and Syngenta. They should collate all their information and prepare a presentation for a class debate on the issue. Give them a clear deadline.

8 On the set date, hold a debate on the potential risks and benefits of GMOs with yourself acting as chair/facilitator. See Chapter 4 for guidelines on setting up debates.

Variation

The techniques in this activity can also be used for debate/discussion about other issues.

Follow-up

Each group writes a report presenting their findings. They can add data from the debate and question the information given. They should account for their opinions and cite their sources.

Worksheet 3.4

Passage 1

Fill in the blanks using one of these words/expressions:
haven't been tested   have been tested   end
be promoted   dangers   benefits

'To leave our children and grandchildren genetically modified foods which .... [1] would be to betray their trust. As we enter the new millennium, millions of women want these experiments with edible crops to .... [2], because we already know that the .... [3] for nature and humanity are too high.'

— Geraldene Holt, food and gardening writer

Passage 2

Replace the words or expressions *in italics* with one of the options below:
are really worried   fewer environmental problems
enthusiastic

'We're *excited* about [1] the potential for genetically modified food to contribute to *a better environment* [2] and a sustainable, plentiful, and healthy food supply. We recognise, however, that many consumers *have genuine concerns* [3] about food biotechnology and its impact on their families.'

— From Monsanto's website www.monsanto.co.uk

Photocopiable © Oxford University Press

Recommended resources

NGO websites and information: Friends of the Earth; Greenpeace; Global Issues; Corporate Watch.

Monsanto website; Council for Biotechnology Information; Agricultural Biotechnology in Europe; Agricultural Biotechnology Council.

3.5 The death penalty

Students express their views on the death penalty and look at which countries retain and use the death penalty. They then discuss some statements from Amnesty International. Follow-ups include research and film viewing.

Level   Intermediate and above

Time   40 minutes plus Follow-up

Aims   LANGUAGE   Speaking, holding a debate.
          OTHER   Reflecting on and discussing the death penalty.

Word store

death penalty execution death row punishment convicted capital punishment offender crime to abolish victim alleged to sentence to condemn

Background information

83 countries still retain and use the death penalty but on average, more than three countries a year have abolished the death penalty over the past decade. During 2002, at least 1526 prisoners were executed in 31 countries. Over 80 per cent of these executions took place in China, Iran, and the USA.

Source: Amnesty International

Procedure

1 Ask students to think for a moment of how they feel about the death penalty.

2 Ask them to express their position by writing either 'for' or 'against' on a sheet of paper and to raise it above their heads.

3 Count the scores and write them on the board, calculate the percentages, and write these on the board.

Example Total in class: 32
Against: 22 = 69 per cent
For: 10 = 31 per cent

4 Ask the students to guess which countries currently use the death penalty. Check against the Background Information box and the recommended resources.

5 Ask the following questions:
a Why do you think these countries use the death penalty?
b Are there any similarities between them? If so, what are they?

6 Ask if the students have seen any films or read any books which address the death penalty, and elicit their names (see recommended resources).

7 Read out the following statements from Amnesty International's website:
- 'The death penalty is the ultimate cruel, inhuman and degrading punishment.'
- 'It violates the right to life.'
- 'It is irrevocable and can be inflicted on the innocent. It has never been shown to deter crime more effectively than other punishments.'

8   Hold a class debate on the issue, using the techniques in 3.4,
    'Questioning GMOs', or 4.12, 'Conducting a discussion'.

Variation

In groups, some students do research into countries that still use the
death penalty, and on cases of people who have been executed
(including those subsequently found to be innocent). Other students
find out the arguments put forth by organizations campaigning
against it, such as Amnesty International. The findings can
contribute to a class debate.

Follow-up

In groups, students watch *Dead Man Walking* and prepare a summary
of the film, highlighting what they think are the most important
moral and ethical considerations.

Recommended resources

Amnesty International's *Facts and Figures on the Death Penalty* at
www.amnesty.org.

The Death Penalty – An American History, by Stuart Banner, 2003, Harvard
University Press, ISBN 0674010833.

Campaign to End the Death Penalty (www.nodeathpenalty.org).

Derechos Human Rights (www.derechos.org).

Citizens United for Alternatives to the Death Penalty
(www.cuadp.org).

FILMS: *Dead Man Walking*, *Last Dance*, *The Life of David Gale*, *The Green
Mile*.

SONGS: 'The Promise', by Johnny Clegg and Savuka.

3.6 Our campaign against war

**This activity makes students think about the impact of a Global
Issue on the people affected. The students do some research and
then plan a campaign, for example, against war.**

Level   Intermediate and above

Time   40 minutes (over several lessons, plus homework)

Aims   LANGUAGE   Using tenses and modals. Oral fluency.
           OTHER   Reflecting about the implications of war.

Materials   Leaflets, booklets and other materials from international and/or
local non-governmental organizations (NGOs).

Procedure

1   Explain the term **non-governmental organization**: a charity,
    association, etc., that is independent of government and business.
    They usually campaign or act to improve a particular issue. Give a
    few examples of international and/or local NGOs (for example,
    Greenpeace, Friends of the Earth, or Amnesty International).

2 Ask the students whether they are familiar with any non-governmental organizations. Ask them to name a few.

3 Tell your students that they are going to create their own NGO, which campaigns on the issue of war (or another issue if preferred). Ask them to think of a possible name for their NGO. What are its aims?

War

- What do you feel about war?
- What are the worst consequences of war?
- Who suffers the most from war?
- What might the benefits of war be?
- Why do we tend to forget about the real consequences of war?
- Has there been a recent war or related event that your country has been involved in?

Photocopiable © Oxford University Press

4 Arrange the students into groups of three or four. Ask them to discuss the following questions:

5 For homework, the students use these questions to interview members of their family or friends about their experiences and memories of war, and their beliefs about it. Alternatively, they can do an Internet or library search on the issue to flesh out their understanding.

6 Ask the students to plan and draft an awareness-raising campaign, with visual elements to help students, teachers, and parents understand better the implications of war. Examples might include posters, competitions using crosswords or questionnaires, talks, workshops, songs, films or film sequences or other media followed by discussion, leaflets, Internet-search competitions, discussion panels, etc. They do the draft in class but finalize the campaign plan for homework, and write it on a poster.

7 Display all the plans and posters and ask your colleagues (or students) to vote for the best one. You assess them too, focusing on feasibility, likely effectiveness, design, etc.

Variation

You or your students can choose a different global issue for an NGO to campaign on.

Follow-up 1

If the school authorities allow, the students implement the winning campaign at school and/or outside, and report on the outcome.

Follow-up 2

Ask the students to research real NGOs' campaigns and to display the information on a large information sheet.

Recommended resources

The Global Issues website

Issue guides on the OneWorld website (for example, arms, genocide, nuclear weapons).

SONGS: 'Peace in the World', U2, 'Bomb da World', Michael Franti. 'Put Down that Weapon', Midnight Oil.

3.7 The classroom for peace

Using some of the principles of UNESCO's Manifesto 2000 for a culture of peace and non-violence, this activity looks at possibilities for action on Global Issues, particularly peace.

Level Upper-intermediate and above

Time 40 minutes

Aims LANGUAGE Reading, oral discussion, using imperatives.
OTHER To raise awareness of individual and group possibilities for participating in global movements; to take individual responsibility for events.

Materials Copy of the UNESCO Manifesto; a copy of one section of the Manifesto per group.

Word store
vulnerable   freedom   **freedom of expression**   manifesto

commitment   **non-violence**   **democracy**

democratic principles   solidarity   **discrimination**   prejudice

exclusion   generosity   injustice   oppression

Procedure

1 Ask the students to take two minutes' silent time, thinking on their own, and to make notes on the following questions:
   a Why is peace important?
   b Try to remember pictures and images you have seen showing life in countries or areas where there is a war going on. How do you think those people feel?

2 Explain to the class that the United Nations has called for a Global Movement to make 2001–2010 the *Decade for a Culture of Peace and Non-Violence for the Children of the World.* Tell them that young people can take part in different ways.

3 Arrange the class into six groups. Each group should choose a scribe to take notes.

4　Give a different Principle Slip to each group and ask them to read it and to discuss its meaning. Ask them to think of examples of actions or attitudes that could support the principle. They should think in terms of their own daily lives at school, at home, and at work. The following questions may be of help:

a　What can you do at home to … (e.g. respect all life, etc.)?

b　How can you defend … (e.g. cultural diversity, etc.)?

5　Ask each student individually to write down their answers in short sentences and then to share them with the other members of their group.

6　Finally, the groups draw up a list of things people should do in order to promote their principle. They should write these in imperative sentences.

Examples　Do not discriminate against others because of their skin colour!
Understand that we are all different.
Respect everybody's right to free speech.

7　Ask the groups to read out their recommendations.

Manifesto Principles

1　Respect the life and dignity of every person without discrimination or prejudice.

2　Practise active non-violence, rejecting violence in all its forms—physical, sexual, psychological, economic, and social—in particular towards the most deprived and vulnerable such as children and adolescents.

3　Share my time and material in a spirit of generosity to put an end to discrimination, injustice, and political and economic oppression.

4　Defend freedom of expression and cultural diversity, giving preference always to dialogue and listening rather than fanaticism, stereotypes, and the rejection of others.

5　Promote consumer behaviour that is responsible, and development practices that respect all forms of life.

6　Contribute to the development of my community, with the full participation of women, and respect for democratic principles, in order to create together new forms of solidarity.

Follow-up 1

Ask the groups to research the Global Movement for a Culture of Peace and Non-violence, and to plan how they might take part, at both individual and group level. Ask them to write a report.

Follow-up 2

The students organize a signature-collecting contest, following the instructions and ideas on the UNESCO website. The group that collects the most signatures for the Manifesto in a given period is the winner.

Follow-up 3

The groups prepare a poster featuring their recommendations and making reference to the principle they worked on as part of the Manifesto for Peace.

Recommended resources

Source: UNESCO International Decade for a Culture of Peace: Manifesto 2000.

Websites: UNESCO; The Peace Foundation; Peace Pledge Union; Cultivating Peace.

WAR: The World Reacts, published by Belitha Press.

'We Want Peace', Lenny Kravitz.
'The Last Straw', REM.

3.8 Say no to racism

Level   Lower-intermediate and above

Time   30 minutes + design time

Aims   LANGUAGE   Reading comprehension. Using imperatives.
           OTHER   Discussing racism and prompting the students to think of possible ways to fight it.

Materials   A copy of the Martin Luther King speech for each student (see below).

Background information

Slavery was officially abolished in the United States in 1864, but black people in that country continue to be subject to discrimination and abuse: they were denied the right to vote until 1965, could not go to the same schools or universities as whites, were paid less for equal work, and so on. Today, racial discrimination continues to be one of the major causes of conflict and suffering in many parts of the world.

Procedure

1   Give out a copy of the Martin Luther King passage to each student.

2   Read out the passage to the class or have a student read it out.

3 Explain the meaning of new or difficult words or expressions, if necessary using the students' mother tongue (for example, 'brotherhood', 'sweltering with the heat of', 'the content of one's character').

4 Explain that this passage is part of a speech Martin Luther King gave in 1963, one year before he was awarded the Nobel Peace Prize and five years before he was assassinated.

5 Elicit how much the students know about Martin Luther King.

6 Gauge the students' reactions to racism by asking:
- Is racism a serious problem?
- Why? Why not?
- Who is affected?
- Have you ever felt the victim of racial abuse?

7 Write the word 'RACISM' vertically on the board.

8 Ask the students to make up imperative sentences beginning with the letters of the word, as in an acrostic.

Examples   R: Reject racial discrimination
A: Accept cultural differences

9 Ask the students to get into groups and design an anti-racism button/badge, using one or more of the slogans provided. They should use their imagination with regard to colours and design.

10 Display the designs and let the class vote for one to be their anti-racism symbol.

Variation

This activity lends itself very well to other Global Issues, for example, war, global warming, pollution, unemployment, globalization, migration, drugs, or corruption.

Follow-up

Start an anti-racism campaign at school, involving not only the students but also teachers and the school authorities. They can use the button/badge design, posters, presentations, videos, etc.

The Speech

I have a dream that one day on the red hills of Georgia, the sons of the former slaves and the sons of the former slave-owners will be able to sit together at the table of brotherhood ... that one day even the State of Mississippi, a state sweltering with the heat of injustice, sweltering with the heat of oppression, will be transformed into an oasis of freedom and justice ... that my four little children will one day live in a nation where they will not be judged by the colour of their skin but by the content of their character.

Martin Luther King

Recommended resources

Racism and Discrimination guides on the OneWorld website.

All Different, All Equal teaching pack published by COMPASS.

Anti-racist Education Pack published by Youth Against Racism in Europe.

3.9 Behind the veil

Level Intermediate and above

Time 60 minutes

Aims LANGUAGE   Vocabulary related to advantages and disadvantages; discussion; presenting a case concisely.

      OTHER   Dealing with stereotypes and prejudice. Promoting cross-cultural awareness.

Materials An enlarged picture of a woman wearing a veil. One copy of the passage per student. Peters' Projection world map (if available).

Word store

Muslim   veil   headscarf   faith   gaze   to prevent ... from

notion   to assert   dignified   chaste   faithful   statement

to symbolize   rejection   western   to argue   to alienate

Procedure

1 Arrange the class into an even number of groups with 3–5 students in each. Label each group A or B. Ask each group to appoint a speaker.

2 Show the picture of the woman wearing a Muslim headscarf (*hijab*) to the class. Elicit what they associate the veil with. How do they think women wearing it feel? Where is it worn? Why?

3 Tell the A groups to list all the possible benefits of wearing a veil. The B groups list all the possible disadvantages.

4 Ask the A group speakers to share their results with the class.

5 Do the same with the B group speakers.

6 The A groups should prepare to present orally, in thirty seconds, one of the good points they found in wearing a veil. The B groups prepare to challenge those points (also in thirty seconds).

7 Ask two A-group students and two B-group students to come to the front of the class and present their 30-second arguments. Repeat this procedure until all the students have presented.

8 Put the pairs of A and B group students who argued together into new groups of four.

9 Give out a copy of the passage to each student and ask them to read it in silence. Help out with any comprehension problems.

10 Allow a few minutes for discussion in groups.

11 Then lead a full-class discussion.

Behind the veil

The Muslim veil, or Hijab, comes from the Arabic word 'hajaba' meaning to hide from view. Codes for wearing the veil vary considerably in different Muslim societies. Some women wear the burka, which hides all of the body except the eyes. Others cover their bodies but leave their faces and hands free; some women wear the Hijab, a scarf over the head and neck.

Wearing the veil is an act of faith, based on the Koran's instruction to men and women to dress modestly. Modern Muslim women argue it protects them from the male gaze and thus prevents them from being sexually objectified. So it is a liberation from contemporary, or western, notions of superficial beauty. Under the veil women feel valued for their intelligence, skills and personality because they do not use their body and its charms for social acceptance.

Modern Muslims in the West speak proudly of wearing the veil because it asserts their identity as faithful, dignified and chaste. This contrasts sharply with the western perception of the veil as oppressive. Over the decades the veil has become a political statement. In some parts of the world it symbolizes a rejection of colonial or western influence. However, some modern Muslim women argue that where the veil has been used to signify weakness, and isolate and alienate women from social life, men have abused their power in the name of religion.

From 'Behind the veil' by Vandna Synghal, in *Orbit* magazine 82, Jan. 2002.

Follow-up 1

The students find out what types of veils are worn in different countries and locate those countries on the world map.

Follow-up 2

In groups, the students identify a garment or a costume representative of their country/ies of origin and note down its symbolism and meaning, and then share this information with the rest of the class.

Follow-up 3

Ask the students to cut out photos from magazines and newspapers showing groups of men and women from mixed backgrounds who have gathered together for conferences, summits, meetings, protests, etc. and to identify the national costumes and their country of origin. Ask them to make posters with labels.

Recommended resources

Understanding Global Issues briefing on *The World of Islam*, published by European Schoolbooks Publishing Ltd.

The A–Z of World Development, published by the New Internationalist.

3.10 What is a home?

Students discuss basic human needs and examine the problem of homelessness.

Level   **Lower-intermediate and above**

Time   **40 minutes**

Aims   LANGUAGE   **Vocabulary to do with houses and homes. Using *would* for likely outcome.**

OTHER   **Raising awareness of the importance of homes and the problem of homelessness.**

Materials   **One monolingual dictionary for every two students; the House chart on p.95.**

Background information

Homelessness has become a serious social problem afflicting hundreds of thousands of people worldwide. Though its causes are complex and there is no single solution, the globalization process is generally understood to be a major contributory cause. One of the social responses to homelessness has been the creation and development in many different countries of magazines and newspapers which are sold by homeless people in the streets of major cities such as London, Seville, Paris, Frankfurt, or Buenos Aires, and also often feature their written contributions.

Procedure

1 Write up on the board the following dictionary definitions of 'house' and 'home':

> **House**: a building that is made for one family to live in
> **Home**: the place where you live or where you feel that you belong

2 Ask the students to take two minutes' silent time, thinking on their own and making notes on the following questions:
   a What turns a house into a home?
   b Why is a home important?
   Make sure the students understand the difference between the words 'house' and 'home'.

3 Now draw the House Chart (opposite) on the board, and ask the students to copy it or give out photocopies.

4 Ask the students to get into pairs but stress that they each need an individual copy of the chart.

5 Elicit the names of the most important rooms.

6 Emphasize the words *physical*, *emotional*, and *social* in the chart and discuss with the whole class what these words mean in our everyday lives, concentrating especially on the difference between *emotional* and *social*. Ask the pairs to discuss the needs that each room helps to fulfil, and to write these in the correct column of the chart.

7 Ask the students to share their responses and write some on the board.

8 Ask them to think about what happens with those needs (emotional, physical, and social) when people haven't got a home (are homeless). It might be helpful to ask them how they would feel if they were homeless.

Follow-up 1

Ask the students to think about how they react individually to homeless people. Discuss in pairs and as a class. You could also organize a role play.

Follow-up 2

The students do research into the causes of homelessness (for example, unemployment, debt, family breakdown, mental illness). Are these factors always the cause of the problem? Or can they also be the effect of the problem?

Follow-up 3

Ask the students to find out if there are any official organizations or NGOs in their country or area working on homelessness and, if so, what actions they take to tackle the problem.

Worksheet 3.10
House Chart

Room in the house	Needs that the room helps to satisfy		
	Physical	Emotional	Social
Kitchen			
Bathroom			
Bedroom			
Dining room			
Living room			
Other			

Photocopiable © Oxford University Press

Recommended resources

The Big Issue magazine.

A–Z of World Development published by The New Internationalist.

'Another Day in Paradise', Phil Collins (see page 121)

Acknowledgements

The definitions are from the *Oxford Wordpower Dictionary*.

This activity was inspired by several of the activities contained in the Crisis educational pack *Changing Lives*.

3.11 Smoke screen

This activity raises awareness about the dangers of smoking and looks at how tobacco companies try to push young people into the habit.

Level Intermediate and above

Age 13 +

Time 80 minutes

Aims   LANGUAGE   Using modals. Discussion. Giving presentations. Reading comprehension.

         OTHER   Awareness of the dangers of smoking and of the tactics used by tobacco corporations.

Materials The article; a set of focus cards per three or four students; at least one monolingual dictionary per group.

Background information:

(According to the World Health Organization), smoking kills nearly 4 million people a year. The WHO predicts that in the year 2020 this number will be 10 million, 70 per cent of whom will be in the **Majority World**. As a result of huge sales losses in the US and Europe, powerful tobacco companies are trying hard to compensate in less developed areas of the world.

Word store

authentic   awareness   tactics   powerful

World Health Organization (WHO)   facts and figures   losses

revenues   compensate   predicts   billboards   youth

targeting   sponsor   community   initiate   field day   recoil

light up   rugged-looking   outfits   clad   imprinted

recruits   brand   emblazoned   to deal with

Procedure

1   Start a class discussion about smoking by asking the students the questions on the next page. Tell the students they can raise any other points they feel are relevant.

2   Read the article aloud with the whole class. Do a straightforward comprehension check.

> a Do you smoke?
> b If you smoke, do you like smoking? Or would you like to stop?
> c If you don't smoke, would you like to smoke? Or do you hate tobacco smoke?
> d Do you think restaurants and bars should have no-smoking areas?
> e Should the government prohibit tobacco companies from selling or advertising their products?

Photocopiable © Oxford University Press

Lebanon lights up

Big tobacco companies must be having a field day. In Lebanon, they have found the perfect market for their products. While westerners are recoiling from the horrors of lung cancer and refusing to light up, the Lebanese seem to be developing ever-stronger ties to tobacco.

All along roads in Lebanon, billboards show rugged-looking men smoking and enjoying the outdoors. Television spots barely take a rest from calling the young to the wonderful world of smoking. On top of that, tobacco companies organize youth activities.

It has become a common sight to see cafés and nightclubs filled with young beautiful women giving out free cigarettes. Wearing embarrassingly tight outfits, the women reward those who light up with sweet smiles. Equally handsome men clad in shirts imprinted with the tobacco brand they represent grin mischievously at girls as they offer them packs of free cigarettes.

It wasn't over yet. The beautiful women then gave out forms for the new smoking recruits to fill in—a fun quiz based on questions about the cigarette brand. Winners received caps and T-shirts with the tobacco brand emblazoned across and of course, even more cigarettes.

Advertising regulations in Lebanon are loose, people are only vaguely aware of the dangers of smoking and—most important—tobacco companies can survive without having to deal with anti-smoking organizations.

From 'Lebanon lights up' by Reem Haddad,
New Internationalist 332

3 Put the students into groups of three or four. Hand out one focus card to each group and ask them to appoint a scribe and a speaker. The scribe should record all their ideas on a piece of paper. The group should help the speaker to prepare to present these ideas to the whole class. Give them time to analyse the questions and to prepare their ideas.

4 Discuss the groups' answers and ideas with the whole class.

1 • How do you feel (if you smoke)?
  • What does smoking do for you/them, according to tobacco companies?
  • Where and how is this view promoted?

2 • Do tobacco companies organize or sponsor activities for young people in your country/area/city?
  • Do they give away free cigarettes?
  • If so, where?

3 • Why have tobacco companies lost huge sales in Western Europe and the US?
  • Why are they targeting other countries?

4 • What is the problem for Lebanese young people?
  • What can be done in order to change the situation, at both individual and community level?
  • What could you do?
  • Who could help you?

Photocopiable © Oxford University Press

Variation

Ask the groups to prepare a news report on this situation. The students should include the opinion of anti-smoking groups, health authorities, parents, and the tobacco companies.

Follow-up

Ask the students to research the dangers of smoking, paying particular attention to information provided by the World Health Organization and smoking or anti-smoking organizations. Statistics and references to their own country should be included if possible. They should present this information in report format.

Recommended resources

The whole article 'Lebanon lights up' appeared in issue 332 of the *New Internationalist* and can be read on their website. Go to the index and search under 'tobacco'.

Article 'Peddling dangerous dreams' on the *New Internationalist* website.

c.o.s.t. (Children Opposed to Smoking Tobacco) website.

who (World Health Organization) website.

3.12 Endangered languages

This activity helps students to reflect on the status of world languages and on the reasons why so many are disappearing from use.

Level Upper-intermediate and above

Time 40 minutes

Aims LANGUAGE   Using imperatives; names of countries and languages.
OTHER   Understanding the importance of linguistic diversity and the rate at which many languages are disappearing.

Materials Worksheet 3.12.

Word store

language **diversity** identity repository knowledge assimilation dominant/dominance attitude

---

Procedure

1 Ask the students what languages they speak. (Speakers of minority languages may not admit to them until later in the activity.) Which languages are spoken in their country/community?

2 Give the students two minutes' silent thinking time to answer the question: *What is a language?* Possible answers might include:
- verbal communication
- a cultural and/or regional identity
- a means of expression.

3 Ask students for their definitions and write a few of them on the board.

4 Give out copies of Worksheet 3.12 and give the students ten minutes to answer it in pairs, and to discuss their answers.

5 Ask for comments and encourage the students to hold a discussion. They might focus on questions such as:
- Why do so many people speak only a few languages?
- Should we care about languages disappearing?

Follow-up 1

In groups, the students do research into a minority or endangered language, either in a country where English is the majority language, or in their own country. How many speakers does it have? When did it start to decline? Can they think of reasons why?

Follow-up 2

In groups, the students debate the pros and cons of speaking a minority language. They can refer back to the definitions of a language in Step 2: for example, can a world language express individual or cultural identity?

Worksheet 3.12
Languages around the world

1 Approximately how many languages are now spoken in the world?
   a Between 5000 and 6000
   b Between 2000 and 3000
   c Around 1000
   d Around 400

2 In which of these countries are there more languages?
   a USA
   b China
   c Russia
   d Indonesia

3 What percentage of the world's languages have fewer than 1 million native speakers?
   a 10%
   b 30%
   c 70%
   d 95%

4 What do the following languages have in common?
   Sámi, Frisian, Breton, Irish
   a They are all Germanic languages
   b They are in danger of disappearing
   c They are official languages in several European countries
   d They all have more than 1 million speakers.

5 What proportion of the world's languages is likely to disappear during the 21st century?
   a 90%
   b 75%
   c 50%
   d 10%

Follow-up 3

The students brainstorm reasons why so many languages are disappearing, and then make a list of possible ways to avoid language death, at government as well as individual and local community level.

Examples of reasons for languages declining might include:
- cultural change
- assimilation to a dominant culture and language
- negative attitudes towards a language
- population movement: speakers become scattered so that the language community breaks up
- economic reasons: a dominant language is needed to get a job and for education.

Answer key
1 a There are approximately 5000–6000 languages in the world, although it is difficult to determine the exact number. For example, the *Ethnologue* counts 27 Quechuan languages in Peru, but the Peruvian government only recognises six of these as languages.

2 d In Indonesia about 670 languages are spoken. It is the second most linguistically diverse country in the world. (The highest is Papua New Guinea, with 850 languages.)

3 d 95 per cent. About 80 languages have more than 10 million speakers. Only a few languages are spoken by more, mostly due to imperialist expansion. The average number of speakers per language is between 5000 and 6000.

4 b They are all in danger of disappearing, as are many other European languages, e.g. Corsican, Occitan, Ladin, Gaelic, Aragonese, Mirandese, Norman, Sorbian …

5 a According to some estimates, up to 90 per cent of languages now spoken will die out before 2100 if current trends continue. According to more optimistic estimates, 'only' 50 per cent will be lost.

Recommended resources

UNESCO's *Red Book on Endangered Languages.*

David Crystal's *Language Death.*

Websites: Survival International; Ethnologue (Languages of the World); Linguapax.

Acknowledgements

The quiz is adapted from one on the Linguapax website.

3.13 Child labour in focus

Students reflect on their daily activities and those of children who work. They then question the justice of child labour by means of a question and answer activity based on authentic material.

Level Intermediate and above

Time 40 minutes +

Aims LANGUAGE Expressions of frequency. Using adjectives to describe a picture.

OTHER Thinking about children's rights.

Materials Cards (see below); picture of an Indian child at a loom (provided); picture of a happy teenager in your country.

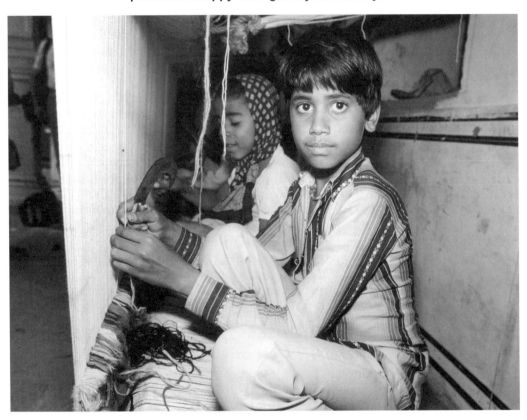

Background information

There are 350 million working children in the world and approximately half of them are involved in some form of hazardous work. They are usually exploited and are denied an education. However, for many families the work of their children is their only way to survive.

Preparation

1 Find a picture of a happy teenager doing something just for fun, or ask the students to bring one each to class.

2 Prepare a number of questions and facts about the issue of child labour (see the Recommended resources) and paste each one on to a separate card. You will need one card per group of students.

Procedure

1 Ask the students what they like to do in their spare time.

2 Tell them to write a list of these activities and note, roughly, how much of their (waking) time is spent on each on a typical day. For example: school: 5 hours, sports: 1 hour, television: 3 hours. Activities could include meeting friends, watching television, reading, writing, sports, listening to music, etc.

3 Show the students the picture(s) of a happy teenager relaxing or having fun with friends. Ask them to describe the picture in detail.

4 Ask them if any of them have part-time jobs. Do they enjoy their job? Do they need to work? How many hours do they work a week?

5 Show them the picture of the Indian child working at the loom.

6 Ask them to discuss the following questions:
   a Have you heard of **child labour**? If so, where and what have you heard about it?
   b Do you think child workers *want* to work? Why? Why not?
   c Do you think a child should have to work?

7 Arrange the class into small groups. Distribute one of the cards you have prepared to each group. Ask the students to read them and to highlight, underline, or point out what they regard as the most relevant items.

8 Ask a speaker from each group to come to the front with a partner. Each speaker should read out a question and their partner should answer it as if in an interview, using his/her own words. The class can comment and discuss each question and answer. (If this takes too long, the students could write comments for homework.)

Follow-up 1

Ask the students to look at the UNICEF website, in particular the Convention on the Rights of the Child, Article 22 (given below for reference). They download or copy it, then write examples of what governments can do to protect children from economic exploitation or any kind of hazardous work.

Follow-up 2

Ask the students to find out about campaigns on child labour and to identify the arguments given by those who say banning child work is not the answer. They bring these arguments to class and then discuss them.

Follow-up 3

Students do some research into the concepts of 'forced labour' and 'sweatshops' and discuss their findings in class.

Recommended resources

Websites: Free the Children; Save the Children; UNICEF
Convention on the Rights of the Child.

Article 22 of the Convention on the Rights of the Child

1 States Parties recognize the right of the child to be protected from economic exploitation and from performing any work that is likely to be hazardous or to interfere with the child's education, or to be harmful to the child's health or physical, mental, spiritual, moral or social development.

2 States Parties shall take legislative, administrative, social and educational measures to ensure the implementation of the present article. To this end and having regard to the relevant provisions of other international instruments. States Parties shall in particular: (a) Provide for a minimum age or minimum ages for admission to employment; (b) Provide for appropriate regulation of the hours and conditions of employment; (c) Provide for appropriate penalties or other sanctions to ensure the effective enforcement of the present article.

3.14 Gender roles and you

In this activity students conduct a survey on who does what at home in order to consider the issue of sexism.

Level   Pre-intermediate and above

Time   40 minutes plus survey time out of school hours

Aims   LANGUAGE   Use of present tense in explaining everyday activities. Arguing a case.

OTHER   Reflecting on and questioning gender role stereotypes.

Materials   One copy of the Household Chores Survey for each student, Gender Statement Slips, a bag or box.

Procedure   **Lesson 1**

1 Ask the students about their families and homes: how many people there are in the family, how many brothers or sisters or children they have (depending on their age), if they have babies, pets, plants, a garage, garden, etc.

2 Give the class five minutes' silent think time to list as many

household tasks as they can (for example, shopping, cooking, house cleaning, changing light bulbs, polishing shoes, changing nappies, bathing babies, washing clothes, ironing, mending the car, weeding the garden, cleaning the garage, etc).

3 Ask them who does each task, and if they personally help in any of them, to say what they do.

4 Tell them that they are going to check their memories by carrying out a week-long survey of who does what at home. The results should be written on a survey sheet such as the example below.

Lesson 2

5 Collect in the survey sheets and collate the results on the board.

6 Ask the students to discuss in pairs what the *balance* is like in their homes. Ask them if there is one person, in particular, who takes on or organizes most of the work, or if the chores are divided amongst the family members. They should also classify the tasks according to gender.

7 Discuss the results with the whole class. If the balance is uneven, can they explain why? Can they suggest ways of redressing the balance?

Household Chores Survey		
Tasks	Done by	How often (once a week, every other day, etc.)
Cleaning the house		
Weeding the garden		
Changing nappies		
Cooking		

Recommended resources

Changing Perceptions, edited by Tina Wallace and Candida March, 1991, published by Oxfam, ISBN 0 85598 137 7.

Taking Responsibility activity pack on anti-sexism, published by RISC, ISBN 1 874709 02 5.

Websites:

WLP (Women's Learning Partnership for Rights, Development and Peace) website

id21 education website

3.15 Human cargo

In this activity students analyse a text on human trafficking and discuss it. There is also scope for engaging with the issue more deeply.

Level Lower-intermediate and above

Time 30 minutes plus Follow-up

Aims LANGUAGE Analysing a text; translation of issue-specific words.
OTHER Discussing human trafficking.

Materials One copy of the passage per student; monolingual and bilingual dictionaries.

Word store

human trafficking   wetback   sex trade   criminal gangs

prostitute   prostitution   to smuggle   to disappear

to threaten   threat   crime   criminal

to force someone to do something   slavery   mafia   forged

forgery   trafficker   to abduct   brothel

Procedure

1 Ask the students what they know about 'Human trafficking' (illegally taking people from one place to another, often against their will).

2 Give a copy of the passage to each student.

3 Ask them to translate the asterisked* words into their own language (or the medium of education). At this stage they may only use a monolingual English dictionary.

4 Check the translations with the whole class, using bilingual dictionaries.

5 Now ask them to translate as many verbs as possible (or other word categories, for example adjectives).

6 Arrange the class into small groups and ask them to compare their results and modify them if they wish.

7 The groups discuss the content of the passage and prepare a brief written explanation.

8 Elicit reactions to the content of the passage. Ask the students if they have any ideas on how human trafficking could be stopped.

Child Asylum Seekers Sold for Sex

African teenagers seeking **asylum*** in the UK are being taken by organized gangs* and sold as prostitutes* in Italy. More than 40 girls, some of them as young as 14, have disappeared* from children's homes in Sussex in the last two years, a BBC documentary has revealed. Police have traced criminal gangs* smuggling* the youngsters to Italy, where they are forced to work in the sex trade*.

Source: BBC News website 8 March 2001.

Variation 1

You can use a text on another topic and asterisk issue-specific words for students to translate.

Variation 2

With higher-level classes, you could use a text in the students' own language and ask them to translate key words into English. This could be a good starting point for discussing any issue.

Follow-up

1 Students find out information on different aspects of human trafficking (for example, child slavery, prostitution, slave workers, etc.).

2 They find news articles on the topic, especially ones with pictures. They can put these together to make a class collage for display.

Recommended resources

Websites (see the Reference library for addresses):

Anti-Slavery International.

BBC News.

Protect Children's Rights action pack by Amnesty International.

4

Music, drama, and communication skills in Global Issues

Global Issues, by their very nature, lend themselves to integrated work. Students naturally work as whole people and tend to appreciate teachers' efforts to integrate subject areas rather than keeping them separate in 'boxes'. In our experience we have had a great deal of success with students' responses, including a change in attitude, and a great improvement in the quality of their work.

In this chapter we look at ways in which you can use drama, music, poetry, choral speaking, making a newscast, student presentations, and projects to explore Global Issues. In some activities we offer a model to work through a particular example, but hope that you can create your own lessons by designing your own materials and adapting our ideas to work with Global Issues you and your students feel are relevant. Issues will change so that what is interesting to one group in one corner of the globe at any one given moment will not necessarily be interesting to another. What is important is that you find your own content (or stimulus point) but deal with it through different media, strategies, and approaches.

Music and songs

Music is a rich and powerful teaching resource. If we choose our materials appropriately (and here we mean that you should consult your students for their tastes and interests as well as using your own favourites), music will not only offer content which is part of your students' world and interests but may also prove to be a springboard to address Global Issues. Pop stars can be very good at raising awareness on different issues. Though their styles and melodies have changed over the years, bands and musicians have sung about freedom, equality, peace, and many other Global Issues since time immemorial.

While songs with meaningful lyrics are rich in content and are often good fun to work with, the value of instrumental music should not be underrated. Under the broad umbrella that covers this type of music we include what has of late been called 'World Music' or 'Ethnic Music'. In addition to 'the flavour of the exotic', it provides a wealth of cultural information on where it originated, and a new perspective, not only on music, but on world views, education, and life in general.

We have included two songs and a model approach for class exploitation plus Internet-sourced information on one artist. The activities illustrate the wide range of things you can do when using songs in your classroom so it will be up to the individual teacher to decide which, and how many, of the suggestions below best meet their class's interests and needs.

With content-rich songs you can:
- identify and discuss the issues
- work on general comprehension
- work with the language
- work with emotional responses
- link to everyday life
- work on background information.

If your students' favourite bands do not address Global Issues in a clear way, you can work with vocabulary (as in 4.7), or you could use the artist as the starting point to discuss a Global Issue (see 4.8).

Content-rich songs: 'Iron Hand'

4.1 General comprehension

Level Pre-intermediate and above

Time 15 minutes

Aims LANGUAGE Reading for gist. Aural and reading comprehension.
OTHER Identifying social messages and Global Issues in songs.

Materials Song lyrics, CD/cassette and player.

Procedure

1 Read the lyrics aloud and ask students to follow the text, making sure they grasp the general meaning of the song.

2 Play the song and ask the students to follow the text.

'Iron Hand' by Dire Straits

With all the clarity of dream
The sky so blue, the grass so green
The rank and file and the navy blue
The deep and strong, the straight and true
The blue line, they got the given sign
The belts and boots march forward in time
The wood and leather, the club and shield
Swept like a wave across the battlefield

Now with all the clarity of dream
The blood so red, the grass so green
The gleam of spur on chestnut flank
The cavalry did burst upon the ranks

Oh the iron will and the iron hand
In England's green and pleasant land
No music for the shameful scene
That night they said they had even shocked the queen

Well alas we've seen it all before
Knights in armour, days of yore
The same old fears and the same old crimes
We haven't changed since ancient times

This song is featured on *Every Street*, 1996, Mercury Records Ltd. (London).

4.2 Time and geographical contexts

Level Pre-intermediate and above

Time 15 minutes

Aims LANGUAGE Reading for clues.
OTHER Placing the events in the song in their social and historical context.

Materials Song lyrics, CD/cassette and player. World map or atlas.

Procedure

1 Ask the students to identify the issue or issues addressed in the song and to try to find a time context for the events described in it. Are there any references to:
   • a specific time-frame?
   • social or musical movements?
   • wars or major conflicts?
   • other specific events?

2 Ask the students to try to identify the geographical context of the song—country, region, countryside/city, area, etc. (In this song, there are references to green grass and 'England's green and pleasant land' which might indicate a country setting—which in fact gives a false impression—see the details at the end of this activity.)

3 Ask the students to locate the area on a map.

4 Ask the students to try to decide whether the situation described in the song relates to a local or a global issue.

5 Ask the students to try to identify words or phrases in the song which indicate the issue that the song is about.

'belts and boots', 'march forward', 'battlefield', 'cavalry did burst upon the
ranks', 'iron will and iron hand'.

4.4

These might indicate the use of force to suppress a demonstration. Your
students are unlikely to know the context of this song: the miners' strike in
Britain in the early 1980s, but they can probably identify similar events. Mark
Knopfler wrote this song after watching a television newsflash about how
the police brutally beat demonstrating miners in the north of England.

4.3 Working with emotions

Level   Pre-intermediate and above

Time   25 minutes

Aims   LANGUAGE Expressing emotions orally.
   OTHER   Establishing links between music, song lyrics, and the
   emotions conveyed.

Materials   Song lyrics. CD/cassette and player.

Procedure

1   Play the song and go through the lyrics, but do not yet discuss the
issues raised.

2   Elicit some words which express emotions, such as *peaceful*, *angry*,
scared. List them on the board (this will give students some
vocabulary to help them describe how they feel).

3   Ask the students whether the song makes them feel anything, either
in general, or whether any lines or phrases in the song have
particular resonance for them or make them feel a particular
emotion.

4   Play the song again and ask the students to imagine what the people
in the song are feeling. Elicit feedback.

5   Round off the activity by asking them which song they would like to
listen to after this one, and how that song might affect their mood.

Comments

This activity should be done before going through the meaning of the
song in detail.

4.4 Working with language

Level   Intermediate and above

Time   30 minutes

Aims   LANGUAGE Vocabulary development, word categories.
   OTHER   Critical analysis of song lyrics in relation to Global
   Issues.

Materials   Song lyrics. CD/cassette and player.

Procedure

1 Ask the students to identify any words and expressions in the song that they do not know.

2 Ask them to try to guess their meaning.

3 Give them time to use their dictionaries to look up the words or expressions. Ask volunteers to read definitions from their dictionaries. Explain the meaning if necessary and elicit other contexts in which the terms could be used.

4 Ask the students to focus on the first verse of the song and to sort words into different groups:

Example colours: blue, green, navy blue
adjectives: deep, strong, straight, true
nouns: dream, sky, grass, rank and file, line, sign, belts and boots, wood and leather, club and shield, wave, battlefield

5 Go through each of the categories and elicit ideas about what these words might represent in this song (for example, belts and boots = the soldiers/policemen, battlefield = the street). Are there any words implying moral considerations? (For example, the deep and strong, the straight and true.) Help out if necessary, but do not insist on your interpretation.

6 See if there is any possibility of sub-dividing the word groups.

Examples • positive colours, negative colours
• adjectives implying something good and something bad
• concrete and abstract nouns
• neutral (sky) and loaded (belts and boots) nouns.

7 Ask the students whether this verse describes:
a a motionless scene
b one with a lot of action
c a scene which is motionless first and then changes.
If they choose the third option, ask them which lines or words suggest the change. Give clues if necessary.

8 Repeat the procedure with other verses.

Variation 1

Divide the class into groups and give each group a different verse. Then bring the whole class together for feedback.

Variation 2

Ask the students to identify which verses fit into the following categories: description, conclusion and reflection, judgement (1 and 2: description, 3: judgement, 4: conclusion and reflection).
Elicit from the class what the message in the last verse is.

Variation 3

Rather than looking at individual words, you can take a more holistic approach and investigate the effect of the combination of words, imagery, and rhythm.

4.5 Links with current affairs

Level   Pre-intermediate and above

Time   15 minutes + homework

Aims   LANGUAGE Speaking.
   OTHER   Establishing links between the song and daily events.

Materials   Song lyrics. CD/cassette and player.

Procedure

1 Ask the students to try to relate the meaning of either the whole song or of one part of the song to an event that has taken place recently.

Examples   • demonstrations where the police or the military charged against demonstrators
   • war between a powerful group or nation and a weak enemy
   • older students bullying younger ones.

2 Arrange the class into groups.

3 The groups look for similarities between the event described in the song and the events they have thought of.

4 Bring the class together to discuss to what extent songs about a particular event remain relevant over time.

Variation 1

Ask the students to look for similar incidents in the news and to bring detailed information to class.

Variation 2

Arrange the students into small groups and ask them to brainstorm on what can be done about it.

4.6 Speaking and writing about the band

Level   Pre-intermediate and above

Time   20 minutes

Aims   LANGUAGE Speaking, writing.
   OTHER   Identifying how artists stand on Global Issues.

Materials   Song lyrics. CD/cassette and player. Background information on the song and musicians. Internet access if possible.

Procedure

1 Elicit from the class the name of the band or musician playing the song. If they do not know, help them.

2 Elicit the musicians' country or culture of origin. Again, you may need to help out. If they belong to a culture perceived as remote or alien, ask students to share whatever they know about or associate with that culture.

3 Ask the students to jot down everything they know about the band/musician, paying special attention to their position in relation to world issues—do they take part in charity concerts? Speak about Global Issues in interviews? Sing about Global Issues? Wear T-shirts with meaningful slogans?

Follow-up 1

If the students have access to the Internet at school, ask them to find information about this band/musician. Is there any information about this song, such as why or when it was written? (This can be done for homework.)

Follow-up 2

In pairs, the students write and prepare a mock interview with the artist(s) with a special focus on their interest in Global Issues.

Comments

1 It is preferable for the students to choose the band/musician, in which case it should not be necessary to help them with information.

2 You could have the information ready photocopied for the students to read. If you have access to the Internet, simply type the name of the musician or band into your search engine and you will have a wide selection of sites offering interviews and information on songs. Relevant information can also be obtained from music magazines sold at newsagents, fan clubs, and CD inserts.

Using students' favourite songs which are not clearly related to Global Issues

Sometimes the lyrics of songs by musicians your students like might not seem to offer much space to work with Global Issues. In this case it is worth searching for some background information about the artist.

When one of our classes decided they wanted to work on songs by the Backstreet Boys, we went through their songs trying to spot one that dealt with issues of wider importance. We browsed the band's websites and discovered that there was a song dedicated to the band's fans in response to their support at a time of great strain for the band. This example is shown in 4.7.

Many popular songs talk about love, which is, of course, an important issue, and the stars themselves could easily be the focus of class work (for example, by contrasting Britney Spears' professed virginity with some of her raunchy videos), but you can also focus on the personality cults of pop stars as 'idols', as in 4.8.

4.7 Working with vocabulary

Level Pre-intermediate and above

Time 40 minutes

Aims LANGUAGE Vocabulary development.
OTHER Reflecting on social problems.

Materials Song lyrics. CD/Cassette and player. Internet access if possible.

Everyone by the Backstreet Boys

We've been through days of thunder
Some people said we don't belong
They try to pull us under
But there we stand together and we're millions strong

Let's get on with the show (let's get started)
Turn the lights down low
You were there from the start
We know who you are and this one is for you

Everyone, everyone
We're standing strong
'cause of what you've done
and this one goes out to you ...

The Backstreet Boys: from the album *Black and Blue*

Procedure

1 Go through the lyrics with the students.

2 Elicit from the class the meaning of the following concepts, helping out if necessary:
Verse 1: 'to go through days of thunder'
'to belong/not to belong'
'to pull somebody under'
'to stand together'
'to be millions strong'
Verse 2: 'to get on with the show'
Alternatively, you can arrange the class into small groups and ask each group to focus on one of the concepts.

3 Ask the whole class who they think the song was addressed to and why.

4 If you have access to the Internet, the students do research on the band in groups, for example, by searching for websites where they can find information on what led the band to write this song. Alternatively, students who like the band in question could bring to class CD inserts or magazines. If they do not have the facilities to find out, tell them that one of the band had serious problems with alcohol and the band was about to split because he could not go on tour with them. Fans showed incredible support for the band and they finally managed to pull through.

5 Ask the following questions:
- When is support from others important?
- How can other people support us?
- How can you support others?

6 Ask the groups to brainstorm some things that could negatively affect their lives and/or careers

Examples drugs, alcohol, family problems, break-ups, money problems, health problems

7 Hold a whole-class discussion about the consequences of alcohol abuse (or any other substance abuse).

Follow-up 1

Ask the class to suggest issues they would like to discuss with the participation of external experts (for example, substance abuse, HIV, human rights, etc.). Make arrangements, being sure to observe school regulations about visitors, and have an open class/debate about the selected issue.

Follow-up 2

Ask groups of students to prepare a mini-project on the making of a CD: writing the songs and thinking of an album title, recording the songs (including where in the world the album was recorded and mixed), designing its cover, preparing promotional posters, writing information on the band members (who plays what and who are the composers) for the CD insert, etc. They can either prepare an example of a publicity poster, or a graphic diagram of the production process. The groups take turns to present their projects. Display the posters on the classroom walls.

4.8 Pop idol

Level Pre-intermediate and above

Time 15 minutes + research time

Aims LANGUAGE Reading.
OTHER Critical thinking.

Materials Internet access or music magazines.

Preparation

If you or the students have Internet access, find a star's website featuring interviews, letters, or comments from fans and enemies alike. Alternatively, look for teenage or music magazines with similar letters. You can ask the students to do this for homework.

Procedure

1 If the students have searched for items, help them decide, perhaps by voting, which passage(s) to discuss first. You may wish to check their suitability for school use first.

2 Go through the chosen passage in class, making sure everyone understands the language.

3 Elicit the students' reactions. If they have contradictory opinions, put them into groups according to their views.

4 The groups discuss the passage and take it in turns to share their ideas with the rest of the class.

5 Ask the groups to swap their point of view: if they were in favour of the ideas expressed, now they should try to think of arguments against them and vice versa.

6 Elicit reactions.

Comments

Many interesting discussions can be sparked by seemingly unrelated issues or, in the case of music, quotes, lyrics, or Internet searches. The main idea is to be able to find workable issues which students can later relate to their own favourite bands/singers.

Example We found the following interview by simply keying in 'Marilyn Manson quotes' in an Internet search engine.

Marilyn Manson's talent for freaking people out has been one of the great success stories of recent years. Unfortunately, it has also created a string of problems for the controversial star. Basically a musician with a flair for the outrageous, Manson has been accused of just about every conceivable ill from invading the minds and bodies of good schoolboys and -girls everywhere to causing otherwise happy, perky individuals to leap off tall buildings in droves.

In the interview, Manson says:

'[In the album *Holy Wood*] I am attacking the shallowness of the entertainment industry, their self-congratulatory attitude, their beliefs that they can never do wrong, that they're always right, that they're the center of the universe. It is a clear attack on the entertainment industry. And I am living right in the middle of the entertainment industry here in Hollywood.'

From 'Interview with Marilyn Manson' by Gabriella, *NY Rock* September 2000

Recommended resources

Music and Song, RBT series, Oxford University Press.

The Rough Guide to World Music, published by the Rough Guides Ltd.

Forty Years of Pop, published by Oxford University Press.

The Harmony Illustrated Encyclopaedia of Rock, published by Harmony Books.

Mixed Media section of the New Internationalist website.

Drama

Drama is a perfect vehicle for students to explore Global Issues. You need very few resources beyond yourself, ideas, and a group of willing students. If, however, you can find a decent-sized space, for example, a school hall, a foyer, dining room, or empty classroom, it will be of enormous help. If not, you can move all the desks to the side of the room, with the chairs neatly placed underneath, and allow the students to sit on them. This will create the biggest space possible in the middle of the room.

More traditional activities tend to take a distanced, academic stance while drama helps students to get inside the issue, inside others, and inside themselves, providing a means to greater understanding. At the same time students grapple with their language competencies in attempting to express their own feelings, ideas, opinions, and the feelings of others.

Students who are actively engaged in the drama of the moment are having to think on their feet and this moment, not any other moment, is what is relevant. Some teachers think drama is just 'mucking about'; however, when well taught and learnt, drama involves thinking skills of the highest order.

Dramathink

'Dramathink' is a way of perceiving real life which has its foundation in the discipline of drama. It becomes practical through following one or more of the ideas listed below, which are by no means exhaustive. What tends to happen is that students will start to create their own original ideas once they get into the practice of 'dramathink'.

It is important to recognise the difference between educational drama and theatre so that the work inside the classroom concentrates not on a minority's ability to perform well for an audience but on the majority's ability to:

- Suspend disbelief
- Be prepared to accept the 'big lie' and to indulge in make-believe as an acceptable discipline inside the classroom
- Work on attitudes rather than characters
- Explore, not an interpretation of other people's writing, but the real, genuine human condition of being inside a dilemma and trying to find a solution
- Use the six areas of drama: movement and stillness, sound and silence, light and darkness
- See drama as essentially a thinking skill in the 'here and now'
- Use students' prior experiences to effect so that every student has a real experience or a related experience to offer and nothing is rejected
- Accept approximations.

Drama is about process rather than product, although you may find that some students need to produce or perform once they feel their work reaches a particular standard. There is nothing wrong in this. In fact it often works as a unifying force and can be highly effective in working with Global Issues.

4.9 Drama on homelessness

The students do a number of warm-up activities before moving on to a role play using cue cards.

Level Intermediate

Time 40 minutes

Aims LANGUAGE **Expressing likes and dislikes. Paraphrasing. Improvising and role playing.**

OTHER **Raising awareness of homelessness and homeless people.**

Materials **A copy of the song lyrics for each student, and a recording of it if possible. CD/cassette player. A copy of the cue cards for each pair of students (see below). A ball (a crumpled-up piece of paper could also be used, or a pair of socks or a scarf rolled into a ball, or a pencil case or a shoe).**

Procedure

1 Read the song lyrics together and discuss its implications. Tap into students' experiences of real life, films they have seen, poems they have read, newscasts they have heard or seen. Listen to their opinions carefully and write up lots of vocabulary and expressions on the board.

2 Have the students sit in a circle if possible. Throw the ball to each student in turn, at the same time asking a question related to the song, and ask them to respond with a word or short phrase. The students can look at the board if they need to.

Examples
- Is the song about a man or a woman?
- Where is the begging person?
- How would you describe the feelings of the man crossing the street?
- What was the begging person's physical condition?
- What worries the woman most?

3 Play the song and invite everyone to sing along.

4 Start with the word *homelessness*. The students sit in a circle and throw the ball to each other. As they catch it, they say a word beginning with each letter of the base word in sequence.

Examples Hate orange man everyone light . . .

Every student should take part orally, even if they only say a couple of words. We are aiming for oral participation and fluency through thinking.

5 Improvisation (optional) If your students are ready for this type of activity, play the song (or read out the lyrics) and ask them to mime the movements, gestures and actions of a character, trying not to act the part but to feel their feelings and understand their attitudes. This should not be ' dramatic' but the students should all be working together at the same time, with nobody watching (or criticizing) anybody else.

6 Role play. Divide the class into pairs (if you have an odd number you should join in) and ask each pair to label themselves A and B. Point to one side of the room and ask all the As to stand in a line with their backs to the wall at one end of the room, and ask the Bs stand in a line with their backs to the wall at the other side so that they are facing each other. In this way you create momentum through movement.

7 Explain that the group on your left is going to play the woman in the song and the group on your right is going to play the passer-by. Re-set the scene in a typical street in your own context and, on your signal, the students play out a dialogue between the two characters. This should be very short and crisp.

8 Stop the action and ask if any pair would like to show their dialogue to the rest of the class. If you have any volunteers, have the pair freeze in position and prepare the class as an audience before they start. Encourage the class to show their appreciation of the effort. Allow as many pairs to present their work as time allows and discuss the good points of the role play after each presentation.

9 Cue Cards: Divide the class into three large groups and ask each group to divide into pairs. Distribute the cards amongst the students. Give them time to read them and ask questions of you, the teacher, if they need clarification for concepts or vocabulary to express themselves. Then, in pairs, but working altogether, role play the parts.

Comments

Teachers may feel that to improvise a dialogue would be difficult for learners without any preparation. However, in our experience students often surprise themselves with what they can do, even if it is very short. They should also not feel that they need to perform.

Cue Card 1A

You are a homeless person living under a bridge. Your clothes are dirty and you are hungry. You walk into town to try to beg for food. Do your best to convince another person to help you.

Cue Card 1B

You are a businessman or woman rushing to an appointment. You are late but a beggar stops you to ask for food. Explain why you cannot help.

Cue Card 2A

You are a homeless person and you decide to enter a public building, such as the Town Hall, to ask for help from the authorities.

Cue Card 2B

You are the receptionist in the foyer of the Town Hall. A homeless person, dirty and in rags, enters to ask for help to find a house. Listen to the requests and respond in suitable ways.

Cue Card 3A

You are a homeless person, sitting quietly on a park bench, reading a newspaper somebody left behind.

Cue Card 3B

You are a young boy or girl, who is angry with the world and on the lookout for trouble. You see a tramp on a park bench and decide to be difficult with him or her. Approach the tramp and find ways of venting your anger on this person.

Photocopiable © Oxford University Press

The song **'Another Day in Paradise' by Phil Collins**

She calls out to the man on the street, 'Sir can you help me?'
'It's cold and I've nowhere to sleep, there's somewhere you can tell me?'
He walks on, doesn't look back. He pretends he can't hear her. Starts to whistle as he crosses the street. Seems embarrassed to be there.
Oh, think twice, 'cos it's another day for you and me in paradise. Think about it.
She calls out to the man on the street. He can see she's been crying. She's got blisters on the soles of her feet. She can't walk but she's trying.
Oh, think twice, 'cos it's another day for you and me in paradise. Just think about it.
Oh, Lord, there must be something you can say.
You can tell from the lines on her face, you can see that she's been there. Probably been moved out of everyplace 'cos she didn't fit in there.
Oh, think twice, 'cos it's another day for you and me in paradise.
Just think about it.

Music, drama, and communication skills in Global Issues | **121**

4.10 Vox populi

This activity is a prepared improvisation. The students role play passers-by in a busy street who are approached by a reporter and cameraperson who ask for their opinions on a specific issue. They take on roles and express the imagined opinions of those characters, as 'the voice of the people'.

Level Intermediate and above

Time 40 minutes

Aims LANGUAGE Expressing opinions. Revising vocabulary, structures, and expressions from previous lessons.

OTHER Playing a role and expressing opinions other than your own. Raising awareness of diversity in opinion.

Preparation

Choose an activity from this book which you have already done in class.

Procedure

1 Write up on the board the title of the activity and underneath it any salient items of vocabulary, structures, or expressions which will help the students remember the activity. Refer the students to any written work they may have done.

2 Ask the students to recall as much of the activity as they can and elicit information and vocabulary. Add any extra points you need.

3 Ask them to imagine that they are walking along a typically busy city street when a reporter, with his/her cameraperson, approaches them to ask their opinions on the topic. They are going to play the roles of reporter, cameraperson, and a number of ordinary people in this busy city street, for example, a businessman or businesswoman, a university professor, a teenager, a senior citizen, a construction worker, a secretary, etc.

4 Divide the class into groups of 5–7.

5 Ask the students to prepare a list of roles and the names of the students playing the roles.

6 Give them 5–10 minutes to brainstorm on ideas as to how each person would play their part; how might a senior citizen's opinions differ from a middle-aged businesswoman's, from a professor's, or from a teenager's?

7 Give the class ten minutes to practise their improvisations. All the groups work at the same time. Go around the groups, helping with ideas, vocabulary, and body language.

8 Ask if any groups would like to present their interviews to the rest of the class. If so, clear a 'stage area' and have the 'audience' sitting comfortably in silence. In turn, each group presents their improvisation to the class. Encourage the 'audience' to applaud their efforts.

9 During the presentations, make notes on the different opinions voiced. Write some of these on the board and elicit others from the students. Ask them how many different views on the same topic they can think of.

10 Hold a discussion regarding the authenticity of the different opinions and emphasize the value of diversity.

Follow-up

Have the students rehearse the improvisations, and video the interviews as part of a newscast on the topic. Show the video to other classes.

Recommended resources

Drama, by Charlyn Wessels, published by Oxford University Press.

Role Play, by Gillian Porter Ladousse, published by Oxford University Press (both in the Resource Books for Teachers series).

See also 4.11, 'Presenting a Newscast'.

4.11 Presenting a newscast

This activity is applicable to all Global Issues and can be done as a one-off lesson or as a longer-term project. The students analyse an authentic recent newscast in order to try to replicate it as a presentation for their own class or for other classes.

Level Intermediate and above

Time 80 minutes plus presentation time for each group

Aims LANGUAGE Analysing newscast format and vocabulary. Listening comprehension. Developing presentation skills.

OTHER Up to date information on Global Issues. Identifying Global Issues in the news.

Materials A video of an authentic recent newscast lasting 15–20 minutes. For Variation: video camera.

Word store

newscast   broadcast   items/stories   current affairs

demonstration   natural disaster   diplomatic visit   talks

meetings   conferences   round of negotiations   accidents

weather forecast   business news   conflict   **coup d'état**

terrorist attack   state   allies   voice-over   location

reporter   on-the-spot   rogue state

Preparation

Either write the questions on the board, leaving about one third of the board for spontaneous notes, or make a copy of the worksheet for each student.

Procedure

1 Show the video of the newscast to the class.

2 Rewind the video to the beginning.

3 Ask the students what they recall from the first viewing and make notes on the board.

4 Draw the students' attention to the questions on the board or hand out the worksheet. Go through the questions to check understanding. Explain that you are going to replay the video, with pauses for them to answer the questions in note form.

5 Replay the video, stopping it regularly to allow the students time to process the information and answer the questions.

6 Discuss the answers with the whole class.

7 Put the students in groups of three. Ask them to choose which of them will be the scriptwriter, presenter, and director for their newscast, and ask them to decide which news item they would like to present. They all suggest items to the scriptwriter, who is responsible for writing; the speaker is the one who learns and presents the script verbally; the director edits the script and gives advice to the presenter from the point of view of the audience.

8 For homework, they prepare the script and practise it as a presentation for the class.

Variation 1

The newscast can be taken 'live' to be presented to other classes or it can be videoed to be shown to other classes.

Variation 2

The groups can be larger if 'outside reporters' are used for 'on location' reports.

Recommended resources

ITN World News video, Oxford University Press.

We the Media, published by The New Press.

Media Awareness and Media Literacy websites.

Worksheet 4.11
Newscasts

1 Who is speaking?

Gender_____   Age_____

Name_____

(Advanced students could also focus on social class and accent).

2 What style of clothing is the presenter wearing?

_____

3 What props has he/she got?

☐ desk   ☐ laptop   ☐ pen   ☐ paper   ☐ file   ☐ notes

☐ autocue

Other _____

4 How does he/she sit/stand?

_____

5 How does the presenter introduce herself/himself, then make contact with the camera/audience?

_____

6 What graphics or other resources are used?

☐ headlines   ☐ photos   ☐ outside reporter

☐ voice-over   ☐ stills   ☐ bullet points

☐ diagrams   ☐ charts   ☐ documents

Other _____

7 What kind of language does the presenter use? (Tenses, active or passive voice, register, length of sentences, complex or simple?)

_____

8 What categories of news items are presented?

☐ international   ☐ local   ☐ weather   ☐ natural disasters

☐ politics   ☐ demonstrations   ☐ elections   ☐ new discoveries

☐ coups   ☐ economy   ☐ the arts   ☐ health and environment

☐ entertainment   ☐ accidents   ☐ crime   ☐ sports

☐ famous people

9 How does the presenter begin, develop, and conclude each item of news?

_____

10 If items are linked, how is this done?

_____

11 How many cuts are there in each item?

_____

12 How many times is the spoken word supported by an image? Does the image match the spoken word?

_____

Communication skills

In dealing with Global Issues we are always dealing with communication between real people. This communication should be both academic and fun. Language barriers create one problem, but really the problem lies within the classroom where we need to **teach** the skills of discussion, debate, negotiation, presentation, critical thinking, creative thinking, reasoning and argument. We are actually talking about higher order thinking skills demonstrated through the oral skills.

Below, we give some ways into starting this kind of work with foreign language learners, who may think this process is too difficult. In fact, it is exciting, and after lots of practice, for both you and the students, you will see a great change in their responses in general and to Global Issues in particular.

4.12 Conducting a discussion

This activity is fundamental to many of the activities in this book. Students are encouraged to develop their skills in discussion and negotiation in order to reach a consensus. It is a matter of constant and consistent practice until the students realize the value of 'academic' debate.

Level Intermediate and above

Time 40 minutes

Aims LANGUAGE Integrating all the skills to hold a discussion.
OTHER Higher-order thinking skills related to Global Issues.

Procedure

1   Ask the students to choose a controversial Global Issue to discuss.

2   Ask them to think about how people should behave when holding a discussion or meeting. Give a couple of examples from the list below.

3   Put the students in pairs and give them five minutes to list as many other factors as they can.

4   Elicit their points, discussing the pros and cons if necessary. Make a list on the board, and add any they have not thought of, discussing each one.

Checklist for behaviour in discussions

- respect
- listening
- turn taking
- processing new information
- waiting patiently
- being relevant, logical, creative, objective
- insisting politely on making your point
- using body language to indicate intent
- always going through the chairperson, at least in the initial stages

---

Photocopiable © Oxford University Press

5   Ask the students to prepare points to make in a discussion on the issue chosen in step 1, bearing in mind how they will make them. They can do this for homework.

6   Hold the discussion. Take the chair yourself at the beginning, and be prepared to prompt when necessary. During the discussion, notice which students might be able to take your place as Chair and relinquish the position as soon as possible.

7   Repeat the process as often as necessary or as indicated in the activities.

Variations

Other possible discussion formats include:
- A **forum**, where four students present their individual views on a specific issue before opening the discussion to the rest of the floor. The audience is given a specific amount of time to ask questions or add comments.
- A **debate**, where two speakers on each side present their arguments, then anyone can ask questions or make points. At the end, a vote is taken. A debate is much more formal and has its roles and rules clearly laid out.

4.13 Teaching presentation skills

The students are shown a bad and a good presentation, and compare them to reach an understanding of the basic requirements of effective presentations. They then try to develop their own skills over a period of time by presenting to their own classmates, to other classes, and finally to an audience.

Level Intermediate and above

Time 40 minutes for introduction. Ongoing slots for development.

Aims LANGUAGE Presentation and structure of arguments. Diction, pronunciation, pace, volume.

OTHER Body language, facial expression, use of gesture, use of equipment to give presentations information.

Materials Visual aids, music, overhead transparencies, posters, etc. Handouts if necessary.

Preparation

1 Prepare two contrasting demonstrations of your own, related to any of the issues in the book. One should be very poor in that you break as many of the rules of presentations as you can and the other as well prepared as possible. Get everything ready before the students arrive to class.

2 Either write up on the board or photocopy the checklist below.

Procedure

1 Show the students the checklist. Go through it and clarify meanings. Tell the students that you are going to give two presentations and ask them to rate you on a scale from 10 for excellent to 1 for very weak.

2 Do the poor presentation and have the students fill in the first column on their checklists. Write their comments and criticisms on the board.

3 Taking their comments into account, do a re-run of your presentation more effectively. Ask the students to fill in the second column of the handout as you present.

4 Ask for comments and sum up the basic differences in the quality of presentations.

5 Have the students work in pairs to choose any Global Issue you have already worked on and prepare two presentations, one good and one poor, to present to each other.

6 Build into your syllabus a continuous process of very short presentations where the students present an issue very briefly each time you use a Global Issues activity: first one minute long, then raise the time limit gradually to 10 minutes, then 20 minutes. Remind the class to use the presentation checklist and have them criticize each other. Over a period of time they will improve so that presenting issues is a natural activity in class.

Presentation skills checklist

	Presentation1 GOOD/BAD	Presentation 2 GOOD/BAD
• eye contact	————————	————————
• facial expression	————————	————————
• hands	————————	————————
• movement	————————	————————
• posture	————————	————————
• use of equipment	————————	————————
• organization of material	————————	————————
• content	————————	————————
• use of visual aids	————————	————————
• pace and rhythm	————————	————————
• diction	————————	————————
• clarity	————————	————————
• volume	————————	————————
• rapport with the audience	————————	————————

Photocopiable © Oxford University Press

Recommended resources

Effective Presentations by J. Comfort, published by Oxford University Press.

4.14 Choral speaking

This activity brings the whole class together in a choral speaking performance. The students work on their understanding of a poem related to a Global Issue and then prepare it as a class presentation, either for themselves or for others.

Level **Lower-intermediate and above**

Time **40 minutes, plus extra rehearsal time if presenting**

Aims LANGUAGE Improving diction, pronunciation, pace, rhythm, changes in volume.

OTHER Thinking about Global Issues. Working together as a team, involving the shy and the reluctant. Raising self-esteem.

Materials Poems and choral speaking guidelines; worksheets.

Preparation

Think about how you will allocate the parts according to your knowledge of the voice timbre of individual students.

Procedure

1 Write the word **choir** on the board and ask if anybody knows (a) how to pronounce it and (b) what it means.

2 Explain that a choir is a group that sings together and that there is an equivalent in **choral speaking** where a group speaks together. Tell the class that they are going to try choral speaking and you, the teacher, are going to be the 'director' or ' conductor'.

3 Hand out the poems with the speaking guidelines and ask a student to read the first poem aloud while the rest of the class read it.

4 Ask the students about the message in the poems. Give out the worksheet below and ask them to fill it in in pairs. Discuss the answers with the whole class and write some answers on the board.

Worksheet 4.14
Who are we?

- Who do you think the writer is? Or what sort of person is he/she?
- How many different types of people does he/she refer to?
- What adjectives are used to describe people?
- What is the poet trying to say?
- Why is he/she saying this?
- What does the poet mean by 'You're all related to me'?
- What do you think of 'strangers', 'foreigners', 'different people'?
- Can you think of one word that sums up the message in this poem?

Photocopiable © Oxford University Press

5 When you feel the students understand the message in this poem, allocate parts according to the guidelines in brackets by the poem, and try out the effects. Only the first stanza has been done for you, and you can change it as you see fit. Take into account the suggestions of the students and practise until the students know their lines and can present the poem as a performance.

6 Record the performance of the poem and play it back to the students. `4.14` Invite comments on the quality of the choral speaking.

7 Give the presentation 'live' to other classes or make a video.

Who are we?

So who are you? *(ALL)*
Are you one of those tall people? *(Group 1—High voices)*
Are you one of those black people? *(Group 2—Low Voices)*
Or are you just one of those people, *(ALL)*
Those other people you know *(The girls)*
Them people? *(An individual student)*
We are calling us disabled people,
Able-bodied people,
Rich people,
Poor people,
Upper-class people,
Middle-class people,
Working-class people, and even
Lower-class people

Who do we think we are?

We call some people
Foreign people,
Strange people,
Different people,
Why do we still label people?
Why do some people feel like chosen people?

OK
I know we come from different places,
We have different shades of skin,
And there are different ways of living
In the countries we live in,
And some people can do some things
And some people can do others
But I think that we have to see
We're all sisters and brothers
And
Children may be small people,
Adults may be big people,
But when you get right down to it
All people are people,
And
As far as I can see
You're all related to me,
That is why I say that
All people are equal.

Now let your reply be true
Everybody
Who are you?

Here is another poem to try if the students enjoyed choral speaking; it can be presented with a reducing cast.

Start with the whole class and reduce the 'voice' until only one person speaks. Essentially the reduction of voices should represent the developing strength of the idea. Of course you can do it the other way round if you wish.

We know *(ALL)*

Monkeys are not doing it, *(ALL)*
Snakes are not doing it, *(reduce the number of speakers proportionately for each line, depending on the number in the class.)*
Neither are beetles or fleas,
Lizards are not doing it,
Birds are not doing it,
They know that we need the trees, *(ALL)*
Mice are not doing it, *(Start reducing again)*
Lice are not doing it,
Cats are not doing it,
Honest, *(ALL)*
Bats are not doing it, *(start reducing again)*
I know who's doing it,
Humans are killing the forest. *(An Individual)*

Both poems by Benjamin Zephaniah, from *Wicked World*, Puffin Books 2000

Recommended resources

Wicked World, by Benjamin Zephaniah, published by Penguin Books.

Dumb Insolence by Adrian Mitchell.

'Old age report' by Adrian Mitchell, 'Prayer before birth' by Philip Larkin, 'The émigrés' by Ted Walker, and 'Open day at Porton' by Adrian Mitchell, from *Contemporary Verse*, edited by Martin Booth, published by Oxford University Press.

Talking Turkeys by Benjamin Zephaniah, (1995) published by Puffin Books.

The Mind's Eye by Alan Maley, published by Cambridge University Press.

Short and Sweet by Alan Maley, published by Macmillan.

Reference library

Arranged by (a) bibliography, (b) educational packs and other teaching resources, (c) teaching resources websites, (d) non-governmental organizations (NGOS), (e) government-related agencies, (f) songs.

Bibliography
Child issues

Green, D. 1998. *Hidden Lives, Voices of Children in Latin America* and the Caribbean. SCF/Cassell/Latin America Bureau. ISBN 1896357148.

Filipovic, Z. 1995. *Zlata's Diary—A Child's Life in Sarajevo*. Penguin USA. AISN 0140242058.

Marcus, R. and Harper C. 1996. *Small Hands— Children in the Working World*. Save the Children UK. ISBN 1899120505.

Consumer issues and environment

Border, R. 1998. *Pollution*. Oxford University Press. ISBN 0194228681.

Border, R. 1996. *Recycling*. Oxford University Press. ISBN 0194228061.

Bramwell, M. 1992. *The Environment and Conservation—A Comprehensive Illustrated Natural History Guide for Young Learners*. Prentice Hall. ISBN 013280090X.

Hopkin, J. and Morris, J. 1987. *Issues in Geography*. Heinemann Educational Books. ISBN 043534580X.

Clayton, C. 1996. *Causing a Stink! The Eco-warrior's Handbook for Kids*. Friends of the Earth. ISBN 0747526850.

Clayton, C. 2000. *Dirty Planet*. Friends of the Earth. ISBN 0704349647.

EarthWorks Group. 1990. *50 Simple Things Kids Can Do to Save the Earth*. Andrews and McMeel Publishing. ISBN 0836223012.

EarthWorks Group. 1989. *50 Simple Things You Can Do to Save the Earth*. Earthworks Press, Berkeley, CA. ISBN 0929634063.

EarthWorks Group. 1991. *The Next Step: 50 More Things You Can Do to Save the Earth*. Bathroom Readers Pr. ISBN 0836223020.

EarthWorks Group. 1990. *The Recycler's Handbook: Simple Things You Can Do*. Bathroom Readers Pr. ISBN 0929634085.

Jacobs, G. 1998. *Linking Language and the Environment: Greening the ESL Classroom*. Toronto: Pippin Publishing. ISBN 0887510922.

Orr, D. 1994. *Earth in Mind: On Education, Environment, and the Human Prospect*. Washington, D.C.: Island Press. ISBN 155963295X

Seymour, J. and Girardet, H. 1987. *Blueprint for a Green Planet*. Dorling Kindersley. ISBN 0863183646.

Scott, M. 1994. *The Young Oxford Book of Ecology*. Oxford University Press. ISBN 0199100837.

Swithinbank, T. 2001. *Coming Up from the Streets— The Story of The Big Issue*. Earthscan. ISBN 1853835447.

Turner, J., Harrison, R., Bingham, B., Binns, R. (eds.) 1993. *The Ethical Consumer Guide to Everyday Shopping*. ECRA Publishing Ltd. ISBN 189817900X

Vallely, B. 1991. *Green Living*. Harper Collins. ISBN 0722524706.

Vallely, B. 1990. *1001 Ways to Save the Planet*. Penguin Books Ltd. ISBN 0140133011.

Wright, D. 1992. *Environment Atlas*. WWF/Philip. ISBN 0540056294.

Cross-curricular ideas

Williams, R. 1989. *One Earth, Many Worlds.* World Wide Fund. ISBN 0947613110. A reference book for teachers who want to work with a cross-curricular approach to teaching global environmental issues.

Discrimination, gender and violence

Wallace, T. and March, C. 1991. *Changing Perceptions.* Oxfam Publishing. ISBN 0855981377.

Globalization and development issues

Brown, L. 2003. *The State of the World.* The WorldWatch Institute. ISBN 0393320820. A yearly report on progress towards a sustainable society

Ellwood, W. 2001. *The No-Nonsense Guide to Globalization.* Verso Books. ISBN 1859843360.

Khor, L. 2001. *The Breakdown of Nations.* Green Books. ISBN 1870098986.

Steger, M. 2003. *Globalization—A Very Short Introduction.* Oxford University Press. ISBN 019 280359X.

UN *Human Development Report.* Published annually by Oxford University Press.

World Bank's *World Development Report.* Published annually by Oxford University Press.

Human rights

Minority Rights Group. 1995. *Voices.* Minority Rights Group. ISBN 1897693958.

O' Connor, M. 2000. *Equal Rights.* Franklin Watts. ISBN 0749626054.

Refugee Council. 2003. *Refugees—We Left Because We had to.* Refugee Council. ISBN 094678759X

Media literacy and the news

Grundy, P. 1993. *Newspapers.* Oxford University Press. ISBN 0194371921.

Hazen, D. and Winokur, J. 1997. *We the Media, a Citizen's Guide to Fighting for Media Democracy.* New Press. ISBN 1565843800.

Music

Broughton, S., Ellingham, M., Muddyman, D., Trillo, R. (eds). *The Rough Guide to World Music.* The Rough Guides Ltd.

Vol.1 (Africa, Europe and the Middle East) 1999 ISBN 1858286352
Vol.2 (Latin & North America, Caribbean, India, Asia, and Pacific) 2000 ISBN 1858286360

Clifford, M. (ed.) 1988. *The Harmony Illustrated Encyclopedia of Rock.* Harmony Books. ISBN 0517590786.

Flinders, S. 1996. *Forty Years of Pop.* Oxford University Press. ISBN 0194228088.

Murphy, T. 1992. *Music and Song.* Oxford University Press. ISBN 0194370550.

Poetry and drama

Booth, M. 1981. *Contemporary Verse.* Oxford University Press. ISBN 0198312431.

Maley, A. and **Duff, A.** 1990. *The Inward Ear.* Cambridge University Press. ISBN 052131240X

Maley, A. 1994. *Short and Sweet.* London: Penguin Longman. ISBN 0140813837

Porter Ladousse, G. 1987. *Role Play.* Oxford University Press. ISBN 019437095X

Wessels, C. 1987. *Drama.* Oxford University Press. ISBN 0194370976.

Zephaniah, B. 1994. *Talking Turkeys.* Penguin Books Ltd. ISBN 0670847860.

Zephaniah, B. 1999. *Funky Chickens.* Puffin Books. ISBN 0140379452.

Zephaniah, B. 2000. *Wicked World.* Puffin Books. ISBN 0141306831.

Various

Burgers, J. 1990. *The Gaia Atlas of the First Peoples.* Anchor Books. ISBN 0385266537. An atlas on indigenous world peoples with loads of facts and references to global issues related to their plights and livelihoods.

Comfort, J. 1995. *Effective Presentations.* Oxford University Press. ISBN 0194570657 (student's book), 0194570894 (teacher's book)

Crystal, D. 2000. *Language Death.* Cambridge University Press. ISBN 0521012716.

Dilts, R. and **Epstein, T.** 1991. *Tools for Dreamers.* California: Meta Publications. ISBN 0916990265

Fisher, R. 1995. *Teaching Children to Think.* Cheltenham, UK: Nelson Thornes. ISBN 0748722351.

Flinders, S. 1999. *The Olympic Games.* Oxford University Press. ISBN 019422872X.

Huxley, A. 1932. *Brave New World.* Longman Study Texts (1983), Longman Group Ltd. ISBN 0 582 33099 8.

Inman, S. and Wade, R. 1997. *Development Education within Initial Teacher Training.* Oxfam. ISBN 0855983906.

Kramsch, C. 1998. *Language and Culture.* Oxford University Press. ISBN 0194372146.

Levine, D., Lowe, R., Peterson, R., and **Tenorio, R. (eds.)** 1995. *Rethinking Schools—An Agenda for Change.* New York: The New Press. ISBN 1565842154.

Phillipson, R. 1992. *Linguistic Imperialism.* Oxford University Press. ISBN 0194371468.

Swithinbank, T. 2001. *Coming Up from the Streets— The Story of The Big Issue.* Earthscan. ISBN 1853835447.

UNESCO. *Red Book on Endangered Languages.* http://www.tooyoo.l.u-tokyo.ac.jp/Redbook/index.html

Unreau, N. J. 1997. *Thoughtful Teachers, Thoughtful Learners—A Guide to Helping Adolescents Think Critically.* Pippin Publishing. ISBN 0887510825.

Windeatt, S., Hardisty, D., and **Eastment, D.** 2000. *The Internet.* Oxford University Press. ISBN 0194372235.

Wright, I. 2002. *Is that Right? Critical Thinking and the Social World of the Young Learner.* Pippin Publishing. ISBN 0887510949.

Educational packs and other teaching resources

Consumer issues and fair trade

- **Fair Trade Foundation.** 2002. *Fair Trade in Action.* Code number 190003. The pack comprises a video cassette, pictures, photographs and activity booklet. Fair Trade Foundation/Reading International Solidarity Centre (RISC). Available through Oxfam and RISC. Please see website section for details.

- **Young, W. and Welford, R.** 2002. *Ethical Shopping: Where to Shop, What to Buy, and How to Make a Difference.* Fusion Press. Code number: 190011. Available through Oxfam.

- **WWF.** 1996. *The Green Consumer Video*—high street shopping for a better environment. WWF-UK.

Cross-curricular ideas

- **DEP.** *Take Part! Speak Out!*—30-page booklet with cross-curricular activities. DEP Manchester, c/o Manchester Metropolitan University, 801 Wilmslow Rd., Manchester M20 2QR, UK. Tel: 00 44 (0) 161 445 2495, Fax: 00 44 (0) 161 445 2360. email: depman@gn.apc.org Website: www.dep.org.uk/globalexpress

- **Edmonds, J.** *Teaching "Environment"*—A video on the management of a cross-curricular theme. WWF UK Education. Available through WWF: Education Distribution Unit, P.O. Box 963, Slough SL2 3RS, Tel: 00 44 (0) 1753 643104, Fax: 00 44 (0) 1753 646553, Website: www.wwf-uk.org

Globalization and global citizenship

- **Birmingham D.E.C.** 2001. *Globalisation: What's it all About?* Tide/DEC and Oxfam. ISBN 164984. Classroom activities and information designed to stimulate and support classroom work on globalisation and the questions raised. Offers links to relevant websites. Available through Oxfam and Tide: Development Education Centre, Gillett Centre, 998 Bristol Rd., Selly Oak, Birmingham B29 6LE, UK. Tel: 00 44 121 472 3255, email: info@tidec.org

- **Christian Aid.** 2000. *Local Citizenship, Global Citizen.* Christian Aid. Code number 165492. Available through Oxfam.

- **Oxfam.** 2000. *A Curriculum for Global Citizenship*—a guide for teachers and education workers. Oxfam.

- **Oxfam.** 2001. *Citizenship Schools.* Oxfam. Code number 161993.

- **Oxfam.** 2001. *Global Citizenship—the Handbook for Primary Teachers.* Oxfam. Code number 164911.

- **Oxfam.** 2000. *Put Yourself on the Line.* A teachers' guide to active global citizenship. Oxfam.

- **Peace Not War** P.O. Box 44212, London E3 4WB, UK E.mail: info@peace.not.war.org www.wewantpeaceonearth.com

- **WWF-UK.** 2001. *A Citizenship for the Future.* A practical classroom guide designed to help young people explore the kind of future they want for themselves, society and the world. World Wide Fund (WWF) UK. Available through WWF-UK. Please see website section for details.

Human rights

- **Amnesty International**. 1997. *Our World, Our Rights*. Amnesty International. This work introduces primary age children to the United Nations' Declaration of Human Rights, and includes guidelines for teachers, games and activities. ISBN 1887204180. Available through Oxfam and Amnesty International. Please see website section for details.

- **Birmingham DEC**. 1996. *Learning to Participate*. Available through Oxfam.

- **Harding, S.** and **Unwin, R.** 1998. *Developing Rights—Teaching rights and responsibilities for ages 11 to 14*. Oxfam Publishing. ISBN 187072724. Available through OXFAM: 274 Banbury Rd., Oxford OX2 7DZ, UK, Tel: 00 44 1865 313770, email: oxfam@oxfam.org.uk., Website: www.oxfam.org.uk

- **Oxfam**. 2002. *Time for Rights*—a teachers' guide with activities for citizenship.

- **Save the Children's Youth Education Programme**. 1997. *Child Labour—an introductory sheet* (free on request from Save the Children).

- **Save the Children**'s *Invisible Children Conference Report*. 1995. ISBN 189912019X.

- **Wessex Publication** and **GLADE**. 1999. *Human Rights and Wrongs*. Wessex Publication and GLADE. Stock code 165468. A unit in a series entitled "Learning Materials for Change"— designed to encourage students to address global issues within their subject areas, published by Wessex Publication and the Global and Development Education Centre (Glade). Available through Oxfam and the Community Resource Centre: 9 Garrett Rd., Yeovil, Somerset BA20 2TJ, UK. Tel: 00 44 1935 433186, email: glade@gn.apc.org

- **Youth Against Racism in Europe**. 2000. *Anti-racist Education Pack*. An activity and information pack written by young people for young people. Available through YARE: P.O.Box 858, London E11 1YG, UK. Tel: 00 44 20 8558 7947, email: yrehq@yahoo.co.uk

Environment

- **WWF-UK**. 2000. *Population and Resources*, a CD-ROM with plenty of useful information about the causes and consequences of natural resource depletion, the growth of world population and poverty, published by World Wide Fund (WWF).

- **WWF-UK**. 2000. *Energy and Climate Change*, a CD-ROM with plenty and useful information on this topic which also offers students a range of views to help them analyse the issue and draw their own conclusions, published by World Wide Fund (WWF).

Various

- **Belitha Press**. 1998. *WAR: The World Reacts*. With case studies, eyewitness accounts and colour photographs, this book helps teachers address the issue of war and provides information on the different ways in which people work to prevent it. Belitha Press. Code number 164178. Available through Belitha Press: London House, Great Eastern Wharf, Parkgate Rd., London SW11 4NQ, UK. Tel: 00 44 171 978 6330, Fax: 00 44 171 2234936.

- **DEP/Panos UK**. 1999. *Global Express* pack and magazine, the rapid response information series for schools on world events in the news. Development Education Programme (DEP)/Panos UK. Code number: 164496. Available through DEP and Panos: DEP, c/o Manchester Metropolitan University, 801 Wilmslow Rd., Manchester M20 2QR, UK. Tel: 00 44 (0) 161 445 2495, Fax: 00 44 (0) 161 445 2360, email: depman@gn.apc.org, Website: www.dep.org.uk/globalexpress

- **European Schoolbooks Publishing Ltd**. 1996. *Understanding Global Issues: the World of Islam*. European Schoolbooks Publishing Ltd. Code number 60962. Available through ESP: The Runnings, Cheltenham GL5 9PQ, UK. Tel: 00 44 1242 245252, Fax: 00 44 1242 224137, email: direct@esp.co.uk

- **New Internationalist**. 1999. *The A to Z of World Development CD-ROM*. The New Internationalist. ISBN: 1869847717. Available through NI: Tower House, Lathkill St., Market Harborough, LE16 9EF, UK, Tel: 00 44 1858 438896, Website: www.newint.org

- **Oxfam**. 2002. *Child Labour—Millions of Children are Being Exploited*. Oxfam. Code number: 190024.
- **Oxfam**. 2001. *Who Rules the World? The UN and the World Bank*. Oxfam. Code Number: 165964.
- **RISC** (Reading International Solidarity Centre). *Taking Responsibility—Internationalist Anti-sexist Youth Work for Young Men*. ISBN 1874709025.

Websites featuring teaching resources and ideas

This section gives the website addresses for resources or organizations listed in the book. The Internet is constantly developing and it is possible that some will change or disappear. If you find any links which are no longer working, or if you have any suggestions, please contact us via the Resource Books for Teachers website www.oup.com/elt/teacher/rbt.

Inclusion in these lists does not necessarily mean that the authors or publishers of this book endorse these sites or their content.

Child issues

BritKid—a website about race, racism and life for teenagers.
www.britkid.org

Childline—Call toll free (UK) 0800 1111
www.childline.org.uk

Cool Planet—Oxfam's website for children and teachers.
www.oxfam.org.uk/coolplanet

C.O.S.T. Children Opposed to Smoking Tobacco—features information and teaching resources related to smoking.
www.costkids.org

Kidscape—plenty of information on bullying and on-line help resource also featuring the Anti-Bullying Campaign.
www.kidscape.org.uk

Success Unlimited—Books and seminars to combat bullying by enriching interpersonal and behaviour skills
http://www.successunlimited.co.uk

The Lion and Lamb Project—a project offering an array of resources, video game and movie reviews, a Parent Action kit, workshops, etc. The project's aim is to stop the marketing of violence to children.
www.lionlamb.org

Development and global citizenship

Development Education Project (DEP) offers a huge array of downloadable teaching resources on global issues and hosts several global projects like for example *Developing Citizenship*
www.dep.org.uk

On the Line—on-line teachers' guide to active global citizenship produced by Oxfam
www.oxfam.org.uk/coolplanet/ontheline

Environment

Agricultural Biotechnology Council A resource service run by the biotechnology industry. Includes a discussion forum.
www.abcinformation.org

Agricultural Biotechnology in Europe A web gateway with links, studies and reports on GMOs, run by biotechnology companies.
http://abeurope.dynamicweb.dk

Council for Biotechnology Information— 'communicates science-based information on the benefits and safety of agricultural and food biotechnology'. www.whybiotech.com

Envirolink—environmental education resources and links on global warming, ozone layer, etc.
www.envirolink.org

Environmental Organizations Web Directory
www.webdirectory.com

Green Teacher Education for Planet Earth Offers ideas, articles and contributions
www.greenteacher.com

Monsanto corporate website promoting GMOs
www.monsanto.co.uk

Redefining Progress—features an on-line Ecological Footprint Quiz and factual information on the impact of human activity on the planet
www.redefiningprogress.org

Endangered languages

Ethnologue—Books, eBooks, and computer resources about languages and cultures of the world for education, research, and reference
http://www.ethnologue.com/

Linguapax—facts and lesson plans on linguistic diversity
http://www.linguapax.org/en/queang.html

Global Issues in general

BBC World Service—English Learning Down to Earth
www.bbc.co.uk
Features ideas and activities for classroom exploitation plus links to other educational sites. BBC News is also useful for information on current affairs.
www.news.bbc.co.uk

Better World Links—a site offering bookmarks arranged per topics—human rights, one world, peace, women, etc.
www.betterworldlinks.org

Cyberschool Bus—a section within the United Nations' website offering classroom activities on human rights, women's rights, health, peace, etc. as well as a selection of games and quizzes
www.un.org/cyberschoolbus/

Disability Now—the electronic version of a British newspaper sharing news, articles and archives about living with a disability
www.disabilitynow.org.uk

Education for a Change
An educational project developed by Ricardo Sampedro to promote work with global issues in the ELT classroom.
www.educationforachange.com

Global Education Web Resources for EFL
An excellent starting point for your search of websites featuring global issues activities and data.
www.countryschool.com/gisig5.htm

Global Gang—a site developed by Christian Aid offering ideas and activities to work with global issues in the classroom. Features interesting 'Teacher Planet' section.
www.globalgang.org.uk

Global Issues—offers extensive information, articles and statistics on all major Global Issues: poverty, arms trade, women's rights, biodiversity, global warming, genetically-modified organisms, etc.
www.globalissues.org

Independent Race and Refugee News Network—in its 'Education' section, the site offers a selection of recent stories on racism and refugees which hit the news as well as a list of useful classroom resources.
www.irr.org.uk

One World—as well as links to over 600 non-governmental organizations, this site offers very interesting fact guides on Global Issues.
Oneworld.net's kid channel features on-line fun and interesting activities for primary students.
www.oneworld.net

Teachers Against Prejudice—a grass-roots organization created by and for educators, students, parents, and concerned citizens to promote understanding and acceptance for all people. Runs an annual essay competition.
www.teachersagainstprejudice.org

The Earth Charter Initiative—features an Education section where you can access their Teaching Resources Archive
www.earthcharter.org

The New Internationalist—one of the outstanding features of this website is a superb section with classroom activities on some Global Issues ('Teaching Global Issues' > 'Easier English issues'). It also has a magazine index arranged by topics.
www.newint.org

The Refugee Council—offers extensive information and ideas on the refugee issue.
www.refugeecouncil.org.uk

WOMAD—the World of Music, Arts and Dance
www.womad.org

Global Issues-related forums

IATEFL Global Issues Special Interest Group (GI SIG)
www.iatefl.org

Japan Association for Language Teachers (JALT)—Global Issues Special Interest Group
www.jalt.org/global/sig

TESOL's Social Responsibility Caucus
http://www.tesol.org/mbr/community

Media literacy

Media Awareness—features a range of teaching activities on media literacy in its *Teachable Moments* section
www.media-awareness.ca

Media Channel—this is a website focused on the media featuring teaching tools, issues and teachers' guides, readings and resources
www.mediachannel.org

Peace education

Cultivating Peace—a website offering information and a wealth of resources to work for peace.
www.cultivatingpeace.ca

Peace Pledge Union—the website of this independent organization of individuals offers in its Education section study and teaching resources on war and conflict, pacifism and non-violence, etc. as well as the texts of several major Conventions and Declarations
www.ppu.org.uk

The Peace Foundation—offers educational peace programmes, resources and information on the International Decade of Peace.
www.peace.net.nz

UNESCO Culture of Peace www.unesco.org/cp

Non-governmental organizations (NGOs)
Consumer issues and media literacy

Ad Busters
1243 West 7th Ave., Vancouver BC, V6H 1B7, Canada
Fax: 00 604 737 6021
email: info@adbusters.org
www.adbusters.org

Clean Clothes Campaign
P.O. Box 11584, 1001 GN Amsterdam, The Netherlands
Fax: 00 31 20 4122786
email: info@cleanclothes.org
www.cleanclothes.org

Consumers International
24 Highbury Crescent, London N5 1RX, UK
Fax: 00 44 (0) 207 354 0607
email: consint@org
www.consumersinternational.org

Corporate Watch
16b Cherwell St., Oxford OX4 1BG, UK
Fax: 00 44 (0) 1865 791 391
email: corporatewatch@org
www.corporatewatch.org

Ethical Consumer
Unit 21, 41 Old Birley St., Manchester M15 5RF, UK
Tel: 00 44 (0) 161 226 2929
www.ethicalconsumer.org

Media Awareness
1500 Merivale Rd., Third Floor, Ottawa, ON K2E 625, Canada
Fax: 00 613 224 1958
email: info@media-awareness.ca
www.media-awareness.ca

Media Institute of Southern Africa
Private Bag 13386, Windhoek, Namibia
Fax: 00 26461 248 016
email: webmaster@misa.org.na
www.misa.org

Media Literacy Centre
3101 Ocean Park Bvd. n°200, CA90401 Santa Monica, USA
Tel: 00 1 310 581 0260
cml@medialit.org
www.medialit.org

Media Rights Organization
104 W. 14th Street, 4th Floor, NYC 10011, USA
Fax: 00 1 646 230 6328
Info@mediarights.org
www.mediarights.org

Tourism Concern
Stapleton House, 277–281 Holloway Rd., London N7 8HN, UK
email: info@tourismconcern.org.uk
www.tourismconcern.org.uk

Undercurrents
16b Cherwell St., Oxford OX4 1BG, UK
Fax: 00 44 (0) 870 131 6103
email: underc@gn.apc.org
www.undercurrents.org

Environment

EarthDay
12718 Northup Wap, Bellevue, Washington 98005 USA
Fax: 00 1 425 556 1095
email: zhprograms@zebrahill.com
www.earthday.com
www.earthday.net

Earthwatch
3 Clock Tower Place, Suite 100, Box 75, Maynard, MA 01754 USA
Fax: 00 1 978 461 2332
email: info@earthwatch.org
www.earthwatch.org

Friends of the Earth
26–28 Underwood St., London N1 7JQ, UK
Fax: 00 44 20 7490 0881
www.foe.co.uk

Greenpeace
Greenpeace International, Keizersgracht 176,
1016 DW Amsterdam, The Netherlands
Fax: 00 31 20 523 62 00
email: supporter.services@ams.greenpeace.org
www.greenpeace.org

Rainforest Action Network
450 Sansome, Suite 700
San Francisco, CA 94111 USA
Fax: 00 1 415 398 2732
email: rainforest@ran.org
www.ran.org

Redefining Progress
1904 Franklin Street, 6th floor, Oakland, CA
94612, USA
Fax: 00 1 510 444 3041
email: info@rprogress.org
www.redefiningprogress.org

World Resources Institute
10 G Street, NE (Suite 800), Washington, DC
20002 USA
Fax: 00 1 202 729-7610
www.wri.org

World Wide Fund (WWF)
Panda House, Weyside Park, Godalming, Surrey
GU7 1XR, UK
Fax: 00 44 1483 426 409
email: wwf-uk-ed@wwfnet.org
www.wwf-uk.org

Fair trade

Equal Exchange
251 Revere St., Canton, MA 02021 USA
Fax: 00 781 830 0282
email: info@equalexchange@com
www.equalexchange.com

Labour Behind the Label
38 Exchange St., Norwich, Norfolk NR2 1AX, UK
Tel: 00 54 1603 610993
email: lbl@gn.apc.org
www.labourbehindthelabel.org

Make Trade Fair
See Oxfam details
www.maketradefair.com

The Fair Trade Foundation UK
Suite 204, 16 Baldwin's gardens, London
EC1N 7RJ, UK
Fax: 00 44 (0) 20 7405 5943
email: website@fairtrade.org.uk
www.fairtrade.org.uk

The Max Havelaar Foundation
Malzgasse 25, 4052 Basel, Switzerland
Tel: 00 61 271 7500
email: postmaster@maxhavelaar.ch
www.maxhavelaar.ch

Transfair Canada
323 Chapel St., 2nd floor, Ottawa, Ontario,
Canada K1N 72Z
Fax: 00 613 237 5969
email: fairtrade@transfair.ca
www.web.net/fairtrade

Globalization and other world issues

Charter 99
18 Northumberland Ave. London WC2N 5BJ, UK
Fax: 00 44 20 7219 3835
email: info@charter99.org
www.charter99.org

Jubilee 2000 Coalition
Cinnamon House, 6–8 Cole St., London SE1 4YH,
UK
Fax: 00 44 (0) 207 407 6473
email: info.jubilee@neweconomics.org
www.jubilee2000uk.org

OneWorld Action
Bradley's Close, White Lion Street,
London N1 9PF, UK
Fax: 00 44 20 7833 4102
email: owa@oneworldaction.org
www.oneworldaction.org

People and Planet
51 Union Street, Oxford, OX4 1JP, UK
Fax: 00 44 1865 245678
email: people@peopleandplanet.org
www.peopleandplanet.org

The Earth Charter Initiative
Earth Charter Secretariat
Earth Council
P.O. Box 319-6100
San José, Costa Rica
Fax: 00 506 249 3500
info@earthcharter.org
www.earthcharter.org

War on Want
Fenner Brockway House,
37–39 Great Guildford St., London SE1 0ES, UK
Fax: 00 44 (0) 207 261 9291
email: mailroom@waronwant.org
www.waronwant.org

World Development Movement
25 Beehive Place, London SW9 7 QR, UK
Fax: 00 44 (0) 20 7274 8232
email: wdm@wdm.org.uk
www.wdm.org.uk

World Social Forum
www.forumsocialmundial.org.br

WorldWatch Institute
1776 Massachussetts Ave., N.W. Washington, D.C.
20036-1904, USA
Fax: 00 1 202 296 7365
email: worldwatch@worldwatch.org
www.worldwatch.org

Human rights and indigenous peoples

Amnesty International
99–119 Rosebery Ave., London EC1R 4RE, UK
Fax: 00 44 (0) 20 7833 1510
email: info@amnesty.org.uk
www.amnesty.org

Anti-Slavery International
Thomas Clarkson House, The Stableyard,
Broomgrove Rd., London SW9 9TL, UK
Fax: 00 44 207 7738 4110
www.antislavery.org

BBC World Service Human Rights
BBC World Service, Bush House, Strand, London
WC2B 4PH, UK
Fax: 00 44 (0) 20 7557 1258
www.bbc.co.uk/worldservice

Campaign to End the Death Penalty
Campaign to End the Death Penalty
PO Box 25730
Chicago, IL 60625, USA
www.nodeathpenalty.org

Citizens United for Alternatives to the Death Penalty
PMB 335
2603 Dr. Martin Luther King Jr. Hwy
Gainesville, FL 32609, USA
Tel: +1 800 973-6548
email: cuadp@cuadp.org
www.cuadp.org

Cultural Survival
215 Prospect St., Cambridge MA 02139, USA
Fax: 00 1 617 441 5417
email: csinc@cs.org
www.cs.org

Derechos Human Rights
Equipo Nizkor
(Derechos Representative in Spain)
Apartado de Correo 156037, Madrid, Spain
Tel: (34) 91-526-7502
Fax: +34.91.526.7515
email: nizkor@derechos.org
hr@derechos.org
www.derechos.org

Food First
398 60th, Oakland, CA 94618 USA
email: foodfirst@org
www.foodfirst.org

MADRE
121 West 27th St., Room 301, New York, NY 10001,
USA
Fax: 00 1 212 675-3704
www.madre.org

Rights Watch
350 Fifth Ave., 34th floor, New York,
NY 10118–3299 USA
Fax: 00 1 212 736 1300
email: hrwny@hrw.org
www.hrw.org

Survival International
6 Charterhouse Buildings, London EC1M 7EY, UK
Fax: 00 44 (0) 20 7687 8701
www.survival-international.org

WLP (Women's Learning Partnership for Rights, Development and Peace)
Women's Learning Partnership (WLP),
4343 Montgomery Avenue, Suite 201,
Bethesda, MD 20814, USA
Tel: (1) 301-654-2774
Fax: (1) 301-654-2775
email: wlp@learningpartnership.org
www.learningpartnership.org

Human development

Action Aid
Chataway House, Leach Rd., Chard TA20 1FR, UK
Fax: 00 44 (0) 1460 67 191
email: deved@actionaid.org.uk
www.actionaid.org

AIDS Action
1906 Sunderland Place NW,
Washington, DC 20036, USA
Tel: 001 202 530-8030
Fax: 001 202 530-8031
www.aidsaction.org

AIDS.ORG
7985 Santa Monica Blvd. #99, West Hollywood,
CA 90046, USA
Tel: 001323 656-6036
www.aids.org

Bread for the World
50 F Street, NW, Suite 500, Washington DC 20001
USA
Tel: 00 1 202 639 9400
www.bread.org

CARE USA
151 Ellis Street, N.E. Atlanta,
GA 30303-2426, USA
Tel: 00 1 404 681-2552
E-mail: info@care.org
www.care.org

Catholic Fund for Overseas Development
(CAFOD)
Romero Close, Stockwell Rd., London sw9 9TY,
UK
Fax: 00 44 (0) 20 7244 9630
email: hqcafod@cafod.org.uk
www.cafod.org.uk

Christian Aid
35 Lower Marsh, Waterloo, London SE1 7RL, UK
Tel: 00 44 (0)20 7620 4444
Fax: 00 44 (0)20 7620 0719
email: info@christian-aid.org
www.christianaid.org.uk

Crisis
Challenger House, 42 Adler Street,
London E1 1EE, UK. Tel: 00 44 (0) 20 7655 8300,
Fax: 00 44 (0) 20 7247 1525,
email: enquiries@crisis.org.uk
www.crisis.org.uk

Free the Children
Suite 300, 7368 Yonge Street, Thornbill, Ontario
L4J 8H9, Canada
Tel: 00 90 5760 9382
email: info@freethechildren.org
www.freethechildren.org

id21 education
The Institute of Development Studies, University
of Sussex, Brighton, BN1 9RE, UK
Tel: +44 (0) 1273 678787
Fax: +44 (0) 1273 877335
email: id21@ids.ac.uk
www.id21.org

Oxfam
274 Banbury Rd., Oxford, OX2 7DZ, UK
Fax 00 44 1865 313770
email: oxfam@oxfam.org.uk
Oxfam@oxfam.org.uk

PANOS Institute
9 White Lion St., London N1 9PD, UK
Fax: 00 44 (0) 20 7278 0345
email: panos@panoslondon.org.uk
www.panos.org.uk

Reading International Solidarity Centre (RISC)
35/39 London St.,
Reading RG1 4PS, UK
Fax 00 44 118 959 4357
email: risc@gn.apc.org
www.risc.org.uk

Save the Children
17 Grove Lane, London SE5 8RD, UK
Fax: 00 44 171 708 2508
email: Publications@scfuk.org.uk
www.savethechildren.org.uk

The Big Issue
Tel: 00 44 20 7526 3480
email: editorial@bigissue.com
www.bigissue.com

Government-related
agencies

UN
United Nations
First Ave. At 46th St., New York, NY 10017, USA
email: unhq@un.org
www.un.org

UNDP
United Nations' Development Program
One United Nations Plaza, 16th floor, New York,
NY 10017, USA
Fax: 00 1 212 906 6596
email: info@undp.org
www.undp.org

UNESCO
United Nations' Educational, Scientific and
Cultural Organization
7 Place de Fontenoy, 75352 Paris 0759, France
Fax: 00 33 145 67 1690
email: webmaster@unesco.org
www.unesco.org

UNICEF
United Nations' Children's Fund
5–7 avenue de la Paix, 1202 Geneva, Switzerland
Fax: 00 41 22 909 5900
email: netmaster@unicef.org
www.unicef.org

UNHCR
United Nations Refugee Agency
Case Postale 2500
CH-1211 Genève 2 Depot
Suisse
Tel: 00 41 22 739 8111
www.unhcr.ch

WHO
World Health Organization
Avenue Appia 20, 1211 Geneva 27, Switzerland
Fax: 00 41 22 791 3111
email: info@who.int
www.who.int

Songs

The **Education for a Change** website includes a
Song Index for ELT teachers, arranged by Global
Issues and students' language level:
www.educationforachange.com/song_index.htm

Bragg, Billy. *Baby Farouk*
Bragg Billy. *The Price of Oil*
Bragg Billy. *NPWA—No Power Without
    Accountability*
Clegg, Johnny and Savuka, *The Promise*
Collins, Phil. *Another Day in Paradise*
Dire Straits. *Iron Hand*
Franti, Michael. *Bomb da World*
Knopfler, Mark. *Imelda*
Kravitz, Lenny. *We Want Peace*
Lennon, John. *Imagine*
McCartney, Paul and Wonder, Stevie, *Ebony and
    Ivory*
Midnight Oil. *Put Down that Weapon*
Plant, Robert. *Network News*
Raman, Susheela. *Woman*
REM, *The Last Straw*
Springsteen, Bruce. *Philadelphia*
Sting. *They Dance Alone*
The Specials. *Free Nelson Mandela.*
U2. *Peace in the World*
Waters, Roger. *Every Little Candle*
Waters, Roger. *Perfect Sense I and II*
Young, Neil. *The Needle and the Damage Done*

Glossary

AIDS Abbreviation of 'Acquired Immune Deficiency Syndrome': An illness that attacks the body's ability to resist infection and which usually causes death

Apartheid Official policy of former South African government which discriminated against black people

Asylum Protection that a government gives to people who have left their own country for political reasons. See *refugee*

Biodiversity The number of different living organisms and the biological communities in which they live. See *diversity*

Bullying Practice through which stronger or more powerful people hurt or frighten weaker people

Child labour Work done by children under the age of 14, usually low paid and in poor conditions, which restricts or damages their physical, emotional, intellectual, social, or spiritual growth as children

Climate change Long-term changes in the Earth's weather and temperature, which have profound effects on all life forms

Communism Political movement in which the state controls production methods on behalf of its citizens. Its aim is to create a society in which everyone is paid and works according to their needs and abilities.

Consumerism The belief that a society or individuals benefit from using a large quantity of goods and services

Coup d'état A sudden, illegal, and often violent change of government

Death penalty The punishment of being killed for certain crimes

Debt repayment Paying back money borrowed from a bank, etc. In Global Issues this term usually refers to *Majority World* nations paying back huge amounts of money to either rich countries or to the World Bank or similar organizations

Democracy System in which all adult citizens have the right to elect the government

Discrimination Treating some people worse than others because of their gender, culture, skin colour, sexual orientation, etc.

Diversity A wide range of different things; the quality of not being the same. See also *biodiversity*

Economic sanctions Restrictions imposed on a country by others or by international organizations such as the United Nations which prohibit trade and aid, and often involve the sanctioned country being denied access to food or medicines

Endangered In danger of disappearing from the world (animals, plants, peoples, languages, etc.)

Environment The natural world in which people, animals and plants live

Equal opportunities A situation in which everyone starts with the same possibilities (of employment, education, etc)

Equality before the law A situation where justice is applied to everyone regardless of their social or economic status

Ethnic cleansing The policy of either forcing the people of a particular race or religion to leave an area, or killing them

Ethnic Refers to a particular racial or cultural group

Fair trade The practice through which producers are paid a fair price for their products and decent pay and working conditions are ensured

Free trade No restrictions or taxes on imports and exports

Freedom of expression Being allowed to say and think whatever one wants

Gender roles Tasks thought to be suitable for men or women in particular (varies according to culture)

Genetically-modified organisms (GMOs) Plants or animals whose genes have been artificially altered, for example, to resist pesticides

Global Issue An issue that affects, or has the potential to affect, a large number of people, animals, or the environment worldwide

Global warming The gradual rise in world temperature caused by an increase in gases such as carbon dioxide which trap the heat of the sun

Global Something which affects the whole world

Globalization The process of integrating the world community into a common system, either economical or social

Greenhouse effect See *Global warming*

HIV Abbreviation for Human Immunodeficiency Virus: the virus which spreads *AIDS*

Homelessness Having nowhere to live

Human rights The basic freedoms that all people should have

Illiteracy Not being able to read or write (adjective: illiterate)

Indigenous peoples Peoples whose ancestors were the original inhabitants of the lands where they live

Majority world A term used to define peoples and nations who are less privileged than the rich minority (replaces terms such as *Developing Nations, the South*, etc.)

Market In a Global Issues context, the state of trade in a particular type of goods. Can also refer to a group of people willing to buy the goods.

Military regime A government run by the armed forces

Minority groups Small groups within a state who are different from the majority because of their race, religion, sex, sexual orientation, language, etc.

Multinational corporations Large, powerful companies which operate in several different host countries. Also known as *transnational corporations*

Natural resources Materials existing in nature, such as water, oil, forests, etc. which are often used as *raw materials* for fuels and industry

Nomads People who travel around and do not settle in any one place for long periods of time

Non-governmental organizations (NGOs) Independent groups or societies which usually work to improve a particular global issue: for example, Amnesty International (human rights), Greenpeace (to protect the environment)

Non-violence Using peaceful methods, not force, to bring about political or social change

Organic food Food produced without chemicals or artificial pesticides and fertilizers

Overconsumption Buying or using too many unnecessary things

Ozone layer A thin layer of gas high above the surface of the earth which helps to protect it from the sun's harmful rays

Pollution Harmful or unpleasant substances (especially waste) put into the air, rivers, etc. which make them dirty and dangerous

Poverty Not having enough of the basic needs of food, clothes, shelter, education, health care, clean water, etc.

Racial equality Situation in which people of all races are treated equally

Racism Discrimination against others because of their race

Rainforest A thick forest in tropical parts of the world which have a lot of rain

Raw materials Things from which something else can be made, in their natural state (for example, wood, rock, ore)

Recycling Gathering waste materials and reprocessing them for reuse

Refugee A person who has been forced to leave his or her country for political or religious reasons, or because there is a war or not enough food, etc. See also *asylum*

Rights See *Human rights*

Sustainability The appropriate and efficient use of resources so that our demands do not damage the environment's ability to support life

Sweatshops Factories where workers work long hours for low pay, in bad conditions, and without access to legal protection

Terrorism The use of violent action for political purposes

The North A term used to refer to rich countries (includes Australia and New Zealand in spite of their geographical location)

The South A term used to refer to poor nations (which in general are located in the Southern hemisphere)

Transnational corporations Abbreviation: TNCs. See *Multinational corporations*

Acknowledgements

Some of the definitions are based on the *Oxford Advanced Learner's Dictionary* and the *Oxford Wordpower Dictionary*.

Index

NOTE: the majority of items are given activity numbers such as 2.11 or 3.13. The few page numbers are in *italics*.